Unhealthy Helping

Unhealthy Helping

A Psychological Guide to Overcoming Codependence,
Enabling, and Other Dysfunctional Giving

Shawn Meghan Burn PhD

ISBN-13: 9781533347534
ISBN-10: 1533347530
Library of Congress Control Number: 2016908484
CreateSpace Independent Publishing Platform
North Charleston, South Carolina

Table of Contents

as her financial health. But when she talked to David about the broken agreements, he became extremely defensive, saying it was her fault he was so damaged. Feeling hurt and guilty, Maggie backed off for a while. Sometimes, he shut down the discussion by saying he was a terrible person suffering from alcoholism and depression. He pledged to do better, and Maggie gave him yet another chance.

Although many cases of unhealthy helping and giving aren't this extreme, Maggie's case illustrates many typical unhealthy helping and giving behaviors. She did things for David he should do for himself, like getting car repair estimates and searching the want ads for a better job for him. When he said he couldn't help his behavior, she accepted his rationalizations and justifications. She softened or removed the natural consequences of his problem behaviors—for instance, driving him around to look for his bike when he forgot where he left it after a night of partying. When he violated agreements, she didn't follow through with promised consequences. She accommodated his addictions when she bought him alcohol and shared her pain medications with him. She over-gave by sharing more of her financial and energetic resources than she could really afford to give.

Codependence

Many people might quickly brand Maggie with a scarlet *C* (for *codependent*). Indeed, the codependent label is regularly used to describe those of us with an excessive and unhealthy tendency to rescue and take responsibility for other people. But the popularity of the codependence notion belies the fact there's disagreement among mental health professionals and addiction specialists on what exactly codependence is, where it comes from, and how to assess it and study it. There are still no agreed-upon diagnostic criteria and it's often defined so broadly that almost anyone could be labeled codependent (including Jesus?). For example, the popular book *Codependence No More: How to Stop Controlling Others and Start Caring for Yourself* by Melody Beattie defines it as having over two hundred characteristics. [3]

That said, therapists, addiction specialists, and researchers believing in the codependence notion generally agree it's characterized by deriving a

One

Understanding the Difference between Healthy and Unhealthy Helping

When her twenty-seven-year-old son David lost his job Maggie invited him to move in with her until he could get back on his feet. They agreed he could stay for up to three months. He'd get a job, pay rent, and do chores. He'd repair his car and get it out of Maggie's one-car attached garage, where it had peacefully reposed for over a year to avoid ticketing.

A year-and-a-half later, David was still there sucking up the oxygen (and the joy) right out of Maggie's home. He was, as my sister Crystal says, his "own crazy little rodeo." Although he had a part-time job as a cook he didn't pay rent or fix his car. He frequently came home in the middle of the night drunk and noisy. He borrowed money from Maggie and burned holes in her furniture when he passed out while smoking. He regularly drank so much he couldn't remember what happened the night before and where his money went. He said cruel things to Maggie when she questioned his behavior. He was even mean to Bob Barker, Maggie's elderly Labrador retriever. Although he was offered a full-time, better-paying job, he declined to take it since it would limit his leisure time.

Maggie frequently had trouble making ends meet, and David's verbal abuse and late drunken hours took a toll on her mental and physical health, as well

Acknowledgements

I'm grateful to the many people who shared their experiences and observations with me, especially my dear BFF Lois Petty to whom this book is dedicated, along with Patricia Winter, Lori Blume, Colin Royall, and my long-graduated student Katie Klein. The many tales of codependence and unhealthy helping and giving shared with me by these folks and others, provide the skeletons of the cases described throughout the book (all names and details have been changed such that the cases are now fictional). I also appreciate those who read early drafts and provided feedback, including Lori Blume, Kelly Moreno, and James Coffey.

My husband, the great clinical social worker Gene Courter also deserves my gratitude. He patiently listened as I shared my ideas on walks with our faithful Labrador companion, Flo (who recently went to retrieve balls and eat biscuits in dog heaven). Gene also deserves credit for sharing his expertise as I hashed out my ideas. Kane Lynch, my son, an enormously productive and creative writer and artist, was also a great source of support and encouragement.

Unhealthy givers often think in ways that make them feel they must rescue others or help and give beyond their energetic and material means. *Chapter 7 The Cognitive Roots of Unhealthy Helping and Giving* examines unhealthy helping and giving through the lens of the *cognitive-behavioral perspective.* The chapter describes a variety of mindtraps like catastrophizing, mind-reading, all-or-none-thinking, personalization, emotional reasoning, and should statements that often underlie our dysfunctional helping and giving. Applying the work of Albert Ellis and David D. Burns, the chapter shows how to question, challenge, and change the maladaptive thoughts that lead to unhealthy helping and giving.

Unhealthy helping and giving have many roots, including culture and gender roles. *Chapter 8 How Culture and Gender Influence Unhealthy Helping and Giving* explains how cultural norms and roles calling for service and sacrifice can be misunderstood, leading to extreme self-sacrifice and enabling. Aspects of traditional masculinity and femininity that promote unhealthy helping and giving are also explored. Chapter 8 also considers cross-cultural differences in unhealthy helping and giving.

If we have trouble saying no or ending unhealthy helping and giving arrangements, we can feel stuck helping or giving even if we don't want to, or know it's unhealthy. *Chapter 9 Healthy Helping and Giving Boundary Setting* is intended to help with what to say and how to say it so that boundary setting works efficiently and effectively, with little or no drama. This chapter also includes suggestions for dealing with boundary guilt, the ambivalence that often arises when we set boundaries and watch others bear their own consequences and struggle to take care of themselves.

Changing our unhealthy helping and giving is no easy feat. *Chapter 10 Final Thoughts on Changing Unhealthy Helping and Giving* explores the personal change process using the transtheoretical model of change, showing how to use it to move from unhealthy to healthy helping. Because ambivalence (that "damned if you do, damned if you don't" feeling) is common when considering personal change, motivational interviewing strategies for managing change-retarding ambivalence are provided. Also included are seven empowering take-away messages from the book.

examines the dynamics of several common types of unhealthy helping and giving relationships including parent-child enabling relationships, unhealthy helping dual relationships, and codependent relationships. This chapter also examines the complications of relationships involving difficult takers. These immature, addicted, or personality disordered people are manipulative, selfish, willing to take advantage, and resistant to givers' boundaries.

The purpose of *Chapter 3 The Negative Consequences of Unhealthy Helping and Giving* is to motivate change by clearly identifying the many negative consequences of unhealthy helping and giving. The chapter details the harms of our unhealthy helping and giving to us, the recipients of our giving, our relationships with recipients, our other relationships, and to our work, family, and household groups.

Some people are "traited" to impulsively rescue, over-help, and over-give. *Chapter 4 The Personality Traits of Unhealthy Givers* considers the role of personality traits and self-esteem in unhealthy helping and giving. Suggestions for managing our prosocial traits so they promote healthy helping and giving are provided.

Unhealthy helping and giving and codependence are frequently motivated by unconscious needs and emotional issues. *Chapter 5 Emotional Influences on Unhealthy Helping and Giving* employs ideas from the psychodynamic perspective. It considers how unhealthy needs arising from unresolved childhood and emotional issues can drive unhealthy helping and giving, and what we can do about it.

Unhealthy helping and giving are sometimes a family tradition. *Chapter 6 Family Influences: Learning Codependence and Bad Helping Habits* applies principles of learning from operant learning theory and social learning theory to explain how some of our dysfunctional helping and giving habits may be learned. The chapter includes a discussion of how unhealthy helping and giving scripts are learned observationally and passed down through families. Another theme is how early relationship attachments create inner working models of relationships that influence later codependence. Chapter 6 also explains how our unhealthy giving is reinforced, how we can use applied behavior analysis to change bad helping and giving habits, and what we can do to raise our children to be healthy givers.

others, their relationships, and for them. Towards this end, the book includes a number of personal change activities. Although these aren't psychometrically validated (in other words, proven by research to effectively do what I intend them to, which would literally take years to do), they are based on standard clinical practice and accepted psychological theories and concepts. If you choose to use the book in this way, feel free to disregard parts or perspectives that don't resonate with you, and focus on the ones that speak to you. And you don't have to use all of the strategies in this book to change; just use the ones that you're willing to try and think will work for you. You're the one that can best determine how the material applies to you and how to craft workable solutions. No one else can understand your situation as well as you can.

Although my intention was to help other people, writing this book also helped me, so thank you very much. A few months into it, I realized that I had my own issues with unhealthy helping and giving. It just goes to show that both God and the unconscious work in mysterious ways. Like many people, I'm sometimes challenged to give to others without unintentionally interfering with their growth or independence, and with my own physical, emotional, and financial well-being. I'm well aware of just how tricky it is to balance giving and service to others with taking care of yourself, and how difficult it is for some of us to set helping and giving boundaries. This insider's perspective, along with my knowledge of psychology, was helpful as I wrote the book. I share some of my helping and giving challenges throughout the book, hoping they'll be useful to you or someone you care about.

Book Overview

Exactly where is the line between healthy and unhealthy helping? How can you tell that your giving has crossed the line? Answering these questions is the goal of *Chapter 1 Understanding the Difference Between Healthy and Unhealthy Helping.* Classic unhealthy helping and giving behaviors and the twelve red flags of unhealthy helping and giving are described.

Human relationships are complicated and helping and giving relationships are no exception. *Chapter 2 Unhealthy Helping and Giving Relationships* individuals, relationships, groups, and societies. Helping and giving to others are sometimes expressions of spirituality and a spiritual pathway. Helpfulness and generosity are character strengths. We *should* help and give to one another. Really, where would any of us be without help from our friends, relatives, coworkers, neighbors, and even the occasional stranger?

Helping others also helps us. Studies find volunteers are less prone to depression, and experience greater happiness, life satisfaction, and self-esteem. Research finds that helping others is correlated with higher levels of mental health, life adjustment, and lower feelings of hopelessness and depression.[1] Helping others may also benefit us by distracting us from our own troubles, improving our moods, increasing our sense of control and usefulness, and reducing social isolation by providing contact with others. [2]

But some helping and giving is unhealthy and unhelpful. This book explores codependence and other unhealthy helping and giving using the psychological theories, concepts, and research that are the tools of my trade as a long-time applied psychology professor and researcher.

My home discipline of social psychology includes the study of prosocial behavior as well as interpersonal relationships, and has many clinical and counseling applications. But I also draw from other psychological perspectives to consider codependence and dysfunctional helping and giving through a variety of psychological lenses. Human behavior is complex so applying multiple psychological perspectives to codependence and other unhealthy helping and giving provides a holistic understanding unavailable elsewhere. Taking a broad view also provides multiple tools for change. That's important because there are many potential causes of unhealthy helping and giving and unhealthy helping and giving relationships vary considerably. That means we need a variety of explanations and solutions.

This book applies psychological theory and research to demystify codependence and dysfunctional helping and giving, but it's also designed to serve as a self-help book or as a tool for therapy. Throughout the book you'll find many practical strategies for personal and relationship change grounded in the art and science of the discipline of psychology.

My goal is to empower people so they can find that giving and helping sweet spot where their help is truly helpful, and their giving is healthy for and go to his counseling appointments, but he won't. And he seems to be getting worse. But he's my father and I have to take care of him. I want to take care of him, I mean it's the right thing to do, but it really limits what I can do with my life."

I could see her resentment rising as if it were a zombie from a grave, her guilt beating it down like a shovel. I suspected this internal conflict was the source of her emotional cave-in. She wanted to be a selfless and giving person but she felt angry and resentful. Admitting this would make her feel like a bad and selfish person so she felt trapped and hopeless. I explained to her how many people in similar situations feel conflicted, stuck, and depressed. "This is probably why your counselor wanted to explore the situation with your father," I said.

After talking a while, she appeared to reconsider her helping commitment. She acknowledged her need to create and enact a new, sustainable plan for her father's care. She agreed that her dad might benefit from a more structured, therapeutic environment like the group home. She seemed to accept the idea that she could still be a loving daughter and a good person even if she altered the helping arrangement and thought about her own needs and future. We talked about some next steps, including the need to continue seeing her therapist, and she said she felt better than she had in a long time. When I saw her some months later, her dad was relocated and things were going well.

I wrote this book for people, like my student, whose giving and helping unexpectedly bring darkness rather than light. Everybody routinely faces decisions regarding whether and how much to help or give, and we often share of ourselves with open and hopeful hearts, as we very well should. Many of our helpful, giving choices end well. But the truth is that few of us get through life without experiencing at least a few challenging helping and giving situations. And for some of us (like parents, highly empathic people, people with codependent tendencies, and those with addicted or mentally ill loved ones), helping and giving challenges are even more likely.

The solution to these common helping and giving challenges isn't to stop helping and giving. After all, helping and cooperating with others is one of humans' most redeeming qualities. *Prosocial behavior,* as social psychologists call it, counters the great selfishness so often seen in people, giving us hope that people aren't all bad. Helping, giving, and sharing promote the success of

Introduction

I wasn't surprised when Erin showed up to my office that day. After all, she wasn't doing well in my psychology class and I suggested she come by to talk about it.

"It's good to see you Erin. Please sit down," I said, gesturing to the couch. "What's up? How can I assist you today?"

She sat down, placing her overstuffed backpack at her feet, her eyes downcast, filling with tears. "I feel terrible about my grade. I usually do so well in my classes. I don't know what's up with me. I have my own business and I'm taking a full load of classes, but I've always been able to do it all, but not anymore. Lately all I seem to be good at is lying in bed crying."

"Mmm…Have you seen a counselor? Do you have any thoughts of hurting yourself?"

"No, I won't commit suicide or anything, and yes, I just started seeing a therapist. I've only seen him a couple of times. He thinks it might have to do with my father but I don't think so."

"Your father?"

"Well, he moved in with me when I was eighteen so he's been with me for about six years. I'm kind of responsible for him."

"I see. Six years, wow, that's quite a responsibility for a young person. What's that like?"

She described him as a violent, substance-abusing veteran she rescued from a group home from veterans with psychiatric problems.

"I didn't want him to live with strangers. I really thought that I could help him and he really wanted out of that home. I thought he'd take his medicine

sense of purpose through *extreme* self-sacrifice to satisfy the needs of others. Codependent people supposedly live for others, feel responsible for others, and don't know where they end and others begin. This leads them into lengthy high-cost caretaking and rescuing relationships they often hold on to despite the costs to themselves or others.

Some theorists also say that codependents are controlling. Melody Beattie, a popular codependence writer, goes so far to say that a codependent person is obsessed with controlling another person's behavior. The idea is that codependent people assume too much responsibility for how others behave, think, or feel. They become controlling as they try to solve people's problems and engineer their change. They tend to get into relationships with troubled, addicted, or underfunctioning people and then try to fix them. In the process, they overlook their own needs, and try to be whatever other people need them to be. Unfortunately, codependent people sometimes attract low-functioning people looking for someone to take care of them so they can avoid adult responsibility, and people in perpetual crisis unwilling to change their lives. [4]

In alcoholic family systems, codependents are often said to occupy the roles of the enabler who protects the alcoholic from the consequences of their behavior, or the hero, who assumes the caretaking responsibilities of addicted family members. [5]

You should be aware that the research on codependence is a bit of a mess. A lot of it relies on questionable measures and methods, and different studies use different measures. Findings are often contradictory and from a research standpoint, most of the studies are of questionable validity.

One of the stronger areas of research focuses on whether codependence is a direct outcome of growing up with an alcoholic or drug-addicted parent. Interestingly, research doesn't support the expected simple, direct link between family substance abuse and codependence. The relationship is weak at best. However, research indicates that emotional abuse and neglect in childhood puts us at risk for the development of codependence. Children who have a parent that verbally assaults, terrorizes, or threatens them; isolates and confines them; exploits or corrupts them; or overlooks, rejects, or ignores their emotional needs appear to be at greater risk for codependence. That's not to say that parental substance abuse isn't a risk factor for codependence because it probably is when it's associated with long-term family dysfunction and emotional maltreatment or neglect. As researchers would say, emotional abuse and neglect mediate the relationship between family of origin addiction and codependence. [6]

Meanwhile, critics of the codependence notion point out that too often, the codependent label is slapped onto anyone (especially women) in an abusive or exploitative relationship (along with other labels like dependent personality, self-defeating personality, or borderline personality). But codependence isn't the only reason we can end up in such relationships, nor is it the only reason we sometimes stay (more on that later). Unhealthy helping and giving sometimes have little or nothing to do with the complicated emotional baggage connected to codependence. It isn't always about the giver's dependence on another's dependence to satisfy their unhealthy emotional needs or about early attachments to difficult or under functioning parents. As you read this book you'll see that unhealthy helping and giving are serpents with many heads. Codependence is just one of them.

Another related complaint is that labeling someone as codependent is too often used in a victim-blaming way, implying that people in relationships with addicts, alcoholics, or abusers somehow deserve what they get. The truth is that codependent relationships often involve challenging situations with difficult people that complicate boundary setting.

Frequently, people labeled codependent are encouraged to consider themselves addicted to relationships with under-functioning others and are told recovery requires a twelve-step program based on the model originated by Alcoholics Anonymous. Although many people find such groups helpful, they aren't the only way to overcome this unhealthy relationship pattern, and this approach isn't a good fit for many people.

There's no question that codependence is a popular concept with at least a kernel of truth, so it's considered throughout this book. For the record, though, I have mixed feelings about the codependence notion. The lack of agreement and contradictory research findings trouble me. I'm concerned how the concept is often used to describe all unhealthy helping and giving. I'm bothered that complicated situations are so often reduced to the giver's codependence. I'm alarmed when people adopt the codependent label and wave it around like a flag of fate. "I'm codependent," some people say, implying this explains everything and they can't change because this is fundamentally who they are. Only adopt this label if it empowers you to understand and change your unhealthy behavior and choices.

Common Features of Unhealthy Helping and Giving

I've said it once and I'll say it again: helping and giving are good. Being a generous, helpful person who goes beyond the helping and giving call of duty doesn't necessarily qualify as unhealthy. The truth is that helping and giving are good for you and contribute to positive relationships, promote individual and group/team productivity, and make the world a better place. It's just that *some* types of helping and giving are unintentionally unhelpful and unhealthy. Fortunately there are clear signs a person's helping or giving is dysfunctional. Unhealthy helping and giving does one or more of the following:

- Enables (promotes) another's underachievement, under-functioning, irresponsibility, addiction, procrastination, or poor mental and physical health
- Breeds false dependence and the need for more help (triggering a self-perpetuating dysfunctional helping cycle)
- Responds to manufactured needs (needs fabricated by the other, or from help that promotes incompetence and dependence)
- Provides a complete solution that reflects the view the other person can't help themselves (dependency-oriented help) rather than partial and temporary help that promotes independence (autonomy-oriented help)
- Greatly exceeds "normal" social expectations for helping and giving in that situation or for that relationship
- Lead to resentment, relationship strain, and relationship conflict

- Negatively affect the giver's physical, emotional, or financial health and are unsustainable

Classic Unhealthy Helping and Giving Behaviors

Let's clarify further by identifying the things people may do that qualify as unhealthy helping or giving. After thinking about this for a long time, I think there are nine basic unhealthy helping and giving behavior categories. Described below with examples, each one embodies some or all of the features of unhealthy helping and giving listed above.

Bearing Others' Negative Consequences

Bearing the negative consequences of others' actions happens when someone behaves in an irresponsible manner that has negative consequences, and we assume those consequences for them. This is a situation where our help buffers others, preventing them from fully experiencing the results of their irresponsible actions. Things like paying their fines, bills, court costs, increased insurance premiums, or late fees, and putting money in their overdrawn accounts, are included in this category. As you might imagine, helping people by repeatedly bailing them out of trouble they brought on themselves can enable their immaturity and irresponsibility. It prevents them from learning the important lessons and skills that promote high functioning. It's often part of a *self-perpetuating dysfunctional helping cycle* where our assistance inadvertently prolongs their need for our help.

Hector is a classic case. He enabled Juan, his beloved 21-year-old son, by paying the increased insurance premiums resulting from Juan's aggressive driving. Meanwhile, Juan continued to drive aggressively and get in fender-benders, partly because the cost of his actions were borne by his father. (I want to say that although Juan was enabled by Hector, Juan is the one truly responsible for his aggressive driving. I don't mean to suggest that we blame the giver for the enabled's poor behavior and choices. My point is only that enabling is a poor use of our helpful and supportive energies because it makes it easier for others to make unhealthy choices.)

Taking Care of Things for Others They Should Do Themselves

A second dysfunctional helping and giving behavior category is repeatedly taking care of things for others that they should be taking care of themselves, or could take care of themselves. Many parents, for example, foster the immaturity and dependence of their children by micromanaging their children's academic or financial lives. They lament their children's lack of life skills and that they must constantly intervene to prevent disaster. They don't get that it's their constant intervention that fosters their children's incompetence, irresponsibility, and dependence. Chapter 2 goes into more depth about unhealthy helping and giving in parent-child relationships.

Doing other people's tasks isn't necessarily enabling them. In healthy relationships we do things to make the other person's life easier or pleasant and they do the same for us—even though these are things we can both do for ourselves. This reciprocal caring promotes relationship health since it meets partners' need to be cared for. Also, doing things for others they can do for themselves sometimes makes sense as a way to divide household labor. For example, one person does most of the laundry but the other does most of the cooking. As long as the balance of giving and receiving is relatively equal over time and there's *mutual taking care of one another*, doing for others is a sign of a good relationship. It's healthy helping and giving.

But doing things for others they can do for themselves is unhealthy when it leads to ongoing imbalance in the relationship (due to one person unfairly doing more of the giving, and the other unfairly doing more of the receiving). That's because unjustified long-term relationship imbalance usually leads to resentment, relationship strain, and conflict (more on that in Chapters 2 and 3).

And, it's also unhealthy if it prevents others from developing or exhibiting developmentally appropriate competencies such that *their independence, growth, or maturity is hindered.* In other words, when our giving acts interfere with another's development such that they're unable or unmotivated to do things that are normally accomplished by individuals at that age, it's unhealthy. Perfectly able people come to count on us to compensate for their skills deficits—deficits that initially arose because we wanted to take good care of them or help them (their needs are *manufactured needs*, because our help created them).

Sandy is a good example of this. Her helpfully-intended support created a self-fulfilling prophecy. When her daughter Samantha graduated from high school Sandy feared a full-time job was too much for her to handle. Samantha had some problems with depression and lacked confidence. So Sandy paid Samantha's living expenses, although she required Samantha work for her own spending money. Now it was ten years later. Samantha still worked only fifteen hours a week and Sandy still gave Samantha money and bailed her out when she overspent. Sandy argued her help was necessary because clearly Samantha was incapable of managing her money, working more hours, or developing a career. But of course Sandy's constant intervention helped maintain Samantha's incompetence. And Samantha herself came to doubt her own ability to be self-sufficient since her mother's actions suggested Sandy didn't believe she was capable. She became anxious and panicky whenever she considered making a step towards independence, which Sandy took as further proof that Samantha wasn't up to the task.

Accepting Others' Bogus Excuses for Poor Performance or Undesirable Behavior

Continually accepting another's sham excuses for under-performance or unacceptable behavior is the third unhealthy helping and giving behavior category. Some of us prefer to believe excuses over the truth because we don't want to think badly of a friend or loved one. We're motivated to justify their behavior to avoid painful realizations about them. Sometimes we feel accepting pitiful excuses is required in our role as supportive parent, friend, or manager. When we see a person's distressed reaction to the negative consequences of their actions, accepting their rationalizations, justifications, and claims of victimization can feel helpful and supportive. Some people find themselves in relationships where they must accept absurd excuses and justifications just to keep the peace. Questioning a sketchy explanation leads to anger and defensiveness and ends in the other person questioning their love or loyalty.

Sixteen-year old Matt's parents provide a typical example. Matt was suspended from school for fighting with his teachers. Rather than face the wrath of Matt, his parents sided with him. They accepted his pleas of innocence and his explanation that the teachers and principal were "stupid" and "out to get him." They supported him in dropping out of school upon which he began a not-so-lucrative life as a video game player, his job prospects (and future) dimmed by his incomplete education and inability to respect authority.

Matt's parents loved him but their support protected him from experiencing consequences that could've promoted his growth and maturity. They also failed to acknowledge and address his problems which ultimately decreased the odds he'd realize his potential. Their help and fierce loyalty sentenced their son to less than he was capable of.

I'm not suggesting we never believe people's explanations for the bad things that happen to them or that we don't ever help people that are in trouble due to their own behavior or choices. Of course there are true extenuating circumstances and explanations that aren't mere excuses. And of course we all occasionally make mistakes and need support and assistance. But that's different from enabling someone's underperformance by repeatedly accepting their questionable explanations. One way to think of it is that when it's a pattern, it's a problem.

Making Bogus Excuses for Others' Poor Performance or Undesirable Behavior

Making excuses for another's poor performance or undesirable behavior is the fourth unhealthy helping and giving behavior category. This is similar to accepting the other's questionable excuses. But in this case, the giver justifies the other person's unacceptable behavior. Some givers fiercely defend their taker to buffer them from others' judgment, or to get others to go easy on them.

Like accepting bogus excuses, making excuses for another's poor behavior is often an expression of loyalty (loyal people defend the honor and public image of friends or loved ones). Also like accepting bogus excuses, it's sometimes a matter of not wanting to think badly of someone we really like or love. For some givers, it's a way to avoid acknowledging what they fear is their own failure as a parent, partner, or mentor. Sadly though, validating another's dependent or harmful behavior by making excuses for it merely prolongs the dysfunction and effectively stunts the other's needed growth.

Such was the case of Lorraine. An older woman with emphysema living on a government pension, Lorraine loved the stuffing out of her youngest son, fifty-year-old Ned. So much so that she paid $5000 bail (her entire savings) to get him out of jail on a domestic violence charge. He promised to pay her back quickly but took an expensive resort vacation making repayment impossible. Lorraine downplayed this, telling concerned family members Ned needed a vacation after his stressful experience. Lorraine even minimized Ned's violence against his wife, insisting it was just a misunderstanding. This was only one of many times that Lorraine defended Ned's questionable behaviors and his poor treatment of her. And it's one reason why it continued.

Covering for Others by Lying for Them or Doing Their Work

Covering for others is the fifth typical unhealthy helping and giving behavior category. This usually involves lying for another or doing their work to keep them out of trouble. Here are some examples:

- A husband calls his alcoholic wife's boss and says she's sick when she's really just passed out from drinking too much the night before.
- To protect his daughter, the parent tells the school official she's home due to illness (the truth is that the parent doesn't know where she is).
- So her son won't be suspected of a crime she knows he probably committed, a mother provides him with a false alibi.
- A woman writes her procrastinating girlfriend's reports so the girlfriend won't flunk out of graduate school.
- A person covers for a friend that's cheating on a romantic partner.
- To help an addicted friend pass a "pee test," a sober friend provides "clean" urine.
- To prevent a slacker coworker's firing, a person takes care of the coworker's responsibilities.

- In a large class, a college student regularly signs in for a friend that voluntarily misses class so the friend's grade won't be negatively affected.

When you cover for others, you may promote their dysfunction by negating or delaying their negative consequences. You artificially diminish a natural consequence of their actions which may enable their undesirable behavior. In the process of covering for them, you often compromise yourself. Covering can set you up for more covering in the future because once you justify covering for another, that reasoning justifies even more covering (what psychologists call the *escalation of commitment* or *entrapment* (more on that in Chapter 3). And, once you enable another by protecting them from the natural consequences of their actions, you can expect more of the undesired behavior, necessitating more covering, and creating a self-perpetuating dysfunctional helping cycle.

Trying to be supportive and helpful, I've covered for others many times, primarily by doing or re-doing their work so they could advance or look more competent than they actually were. The first time I remember doing this was in college. I was a server at a restaurant and worked a shift with Cliff. Cliff was at best a terrible waiter and I covered for him constantly by taking care of his tables and his side work. The truth is, Cliff didn't meet his responsibilities but management had no idea because I worked hard enough for the both of us. It wasn't fair but it was my fault; I set the whole thing in motion by voluntarily starting to cover for him.

Eventually though, I felt irritated and stuck. I didn't want to rat out a friend because I didn't want him to get in trouble, and I didn't know how to change the relationship pattern I helped create. Now much older and a wee bit wiser, I see I had other choices. I could've asserted myself and stopped covering for him. I could've lowered my standards and accepted that some customers would receive less-than-perfect service. Also, in retrospect I see that if I hadn't covered for him, a manager might have addressed his weak performance. Or, if I didn't intervene, perhaps poor tips would have motivated his improvement. So you see, I probably didn't need to take care of it; it would have taken care of itself, no martyrdom required.

While in some ways the loyalty that leads to covering for friends or loved one is admirable and reflects positively on a giver's character, covering is usually misplaced loyalty that creates problems, including the erosion of the giver's integrity. If caught, both the giver and the recipient are likely to face unpleasant consequences, especially if the covering involved lying to authorities. Depending on the nature of the covering, negative consequences may include anger from those deceived, damage to the giver's reputation due to dishonesty, employment termination, or legal charges such as obstruction of justice or aiding and abetting criminal or unethical behavior.

Of course, there are circumstances under which covering for others is warranted. For example, I think most people would agree that Miep Gies, the Dutch woman who along with four others, concealed Ann Frank and her family from the Nazis in the occupied Netherlands, acted heroically and ethically when she covered for the Frank family.

Overlooking Violated Boundaries and Agreements

The sixth unhealthy helping and giving behavior category is overlooking violated boundaries and agreements. In many dysfunctional helping and giving relationships, boundaries are set by the giver and then pushed by the taker. Deadlines are missed with little fanfare, agreements aren't upheld, and ultimatums are empty threats. Examples include:

- The spouse that regularly says, "If you come home loaded again, I'm leaving you!" and never does
- The parent that says his adult son can stay with him for three months if he gets a job and saves money, but when the son chooses not to, fails to enforce the agreement
- The person that answers a friend's multiple daily calls, although they agreed the calling was excessive and to be limited to one call a day
- The manager who gives a poorly performing employee yet another chance to get help for an addiction and improve their job performance, even though the employee has yet to consistently adhere to any agreements

- The adult grandchild that pays the grandfather's bills resulting from compulsive gambling, although the grandfather failed to get the treatment agreed upon as a condition of the last bailout

Failing to enforce agreements often enables other people. People learn to make peace with us by listening and agreeing with our boundaries and agreements. Meanwhile, they know from experience we're unlikely to follow through. Or, even if they had good intentions when they made an agreement, they're lured away by the siren song of their old habits. When a slip is met with none of the threatened consequences, the old, established behavior patterns continue with nary a hiccup. Chapter 6 explains in more detail how unhealthy givers often reinforce takers' undesired behaviors by not following through with previously agreed-upon consequences.

Accommodating Others' Unhealthy Behavior

The seventh unhealthy helping and giving behavior is accommodating another's unhealthy behavior. This behavior is particularly common in unhealthy helping and giving relationships involving the enabling of psychiatric disorders, physical illnesses, and addictions. The giver demonstrates caring and love by helpfully catering to manufactured needs arising from a poorly managed mental or physical health condition or addiction, needs that would be non-existent if the person sought treatment or stuck to a prescribed treatment plan or program. Here are some typical examples of accommodation:

- For five years, a daughter has helped her mother (who has obsessive-compulsive disorder) complete exhaustive daily cleaning rituals
- A man puts up with increasing levels of disorder and loss of space in his home due to his partner's hoarding
- A woman takes care of her neighbor's grocery shopping so the neighbor (who suffers from agoraphobia) doesn't have to leave the house. Originally, the woman would go with her to the store, but now she won't do even that

- A daughter's eating disorder (anorexia) is enabled when her parents cater to her many "rules" for meals (such as weighing out portions and cutting her food into small pieces)
- The wife of a man with a compulsive eating disorder stocks the pantry with his favorite items for bingeing and caters to him by cooking massive quantities of food. He's now so overweight he cannot work
- A man enables his son's addiction by driving him to his drug connection so he can score
- A wife keeps the refrigerator stocked with beer for her alcoholic husband

Of course, accommodating these manufactured needs only enables the disorder or addiction because it makes it easier for the other to continue doing the things that feed it. Long-term accommodation may worsen their condition and make it even more difficult for them to change (because over time, bad habits become more entrenched and they have farther to go to get better). Once they deteriorate and suffer, it becomes even harder for givers to step away in yet another self-perpetuating dysfunctional helping cycle. This is one reason why treatment programs for addiction and eating disorders often have a family treatment component. They know that these conditions are sometimes part of an enabling family system that includes accommodation and other dysfunctional helping and giving behaviors.

It's important to understand that when dependency arises out of an honest, true need for assistance, like that arising from disability or developmental stage, it's very different from the dependency of the unhealthy helping relationship. If you're injured or hurt, or disabled, you may be dependent on other people to care for you. If you're my baby, or if you're my 100-year-old mother, your dependence on me is appropriate and understandable (and so is my caregiving towards you). This is quite different from the dependencies seen in dysfunctional helping relationships, dependencies that are essentially conjured up or magnified by one or both parties.

Other forms of helpful accommodation may also qualify as unhealthy if they deplete the giver's resources. Some people work so hard to accommodate everyone that they burn themselves out. For example, as a mother and hostess, my excessive efforts to accommodate everyone's unique food preferences significantly added to my stress and workload. As a teacher, leader, and manager, my efforts to listen to and accommodate group members' unique perspectives and needs exhausted me. Fortunately, I'm finally learning how to kick my accommodating behaviors down a notch to preserve my health and sanity.

Rescuing Others

The eighth typical unhealthy helping and giving behavior is rescuing. Rescuing includes the impulsive offering of aid in response to another's difficulty. Of course, this isn't always a bad thing. My husband, for example, has rescued several people from burning or overturned cars, and he's prevented a suicidal person from jumping off a bridge. However, some people are habitual unhealthy rescuers, often rescuing when rescue is unnecessary or ill advised. They rescue when others will be fine without their intervention or weren't even asking for a rescue. They rescue people that use them to escape responsibility. They rescue in ways that are ultimately unsustainable. They rescue people who probably shouldn't be rescued because they could benefit from handling their own problems.

People that launch unhealthy rescues may impulsively offer financial assistance they can't afford. They may invite others to live with them despite limited space and resources. Or they volunteer to help people with tasks or errands when they don't have enough time or energy to take care of their own responsibilities. Unhealthy rescuers often rashly make promises of help they later regret.

Some rescuers jump in to fix other people's complicated problems or relationships only to feel frustrated when people don't welcome their advice or won't follow their recommendations. Unhealthy rescuers often become physically, emotionally, and financially stressed as a result of their impetuous efforts to help. Fiona, for example, impulsively rescued so many stray cats and dogs that she faced financial ruin and was unable to properly care for all of them. Unhealthy rescuers in professional helping roles rashly offer assistance that violates professional boundaries and endangers themselves, others, or their career. Chapter 4 explains that rescuing is particularly common among people high in empathy. These folks experience others' distress almost as if it were their own and feel compelled to do something so that everyone can feel better.

Over-Helping/Over-Giving

Over-helping and over-giving is the final unhealthy helping and giving behavior category. People who over-help go beyond the helping call of duty, exceeding the level of task help that's normally provided in a particular type of situation or in that type of relationship. Over-helpers want to be helpful and supportive to a group or individual so they take on more chores, errands, and responsibilities than is necessary, expected, or fair. Over-helping also includes the excessive giving of unsolicited (and usually unwanted) advice and task assistance (this type of help is called *assumptive help*).

People that over-help often do more than their share of work in groups, taking on more responsibility than is truly theirs. For instance, in a work or volunteer group they take on many more tasks than other group members. They do more than their fair share of the labor at holiday and group gatherings. In a roommate or family living situation, they're the responsible ones that clean up more than others, buy more food and toilet paper, and make sure that bills are paid. Some helpers are over-the-top with their helpfulness in multiple relationships (friends, neighbors, family members, work) and multiple settings (home, work, volunteer, etc.).

Over-givers often have one-sided relationships where they give at a much higher level than their relationship partners, or give more than is appropriate for that type of relationship. They're often so giving that they become doormats that regularly subvert their own needs and desires to give what other people need, want, or demand. They often end up wondering whether people really like them or just like what they can get from them. Many are unassertive and don't stand up for themselves or know how to say no to requests for their time, money, or assistance.

One big problem with over-helping and over-giving is that they're ultimately unsustainable, either financially or energetically. Extreme helping and giving can lead to burnout, a type of physical and emotional exhaustion. Eventually the helper becomes so run down they find it difficult to continue their high level of service to others. And of course, over-helping can enable others' incompetence, procrastination, and irresponsibility, which only makes us over-help some more, promoting further incompetence, irresponsibility, and so on, creating a self-perpetuating dysfunctional helping cycle. These harms are discussed in more detail in Chapter 3.

Another problem is that over-helping and over-giving can unexpectedly harm our relationships. You'll read more about these dynamics in Chapters 2 and 3. For now let's just say that although helpers and givers often expect their generosity and intervention to strengthen their relationships and lead others to like them, the outcome is sometimes the opposite. That's because over-helping and over-giving create relationship imbalance (and a host of relationship problems), and are often misperceived as controlling and judgmental. For example, recipients of unsolicited advice often experience it as disrespectful and irritating. Recipients of over-giving often experience uncomfortable feelings because they can't reciprocate, feel forced to reciprocate, or because they perceive the gifts as a reminder of their lack of success. Over-givers are then hurt by what feels like a lack of appreciation.

Use Box 1.1 to think about your unhealthy helping and giving behaviors.

Box 1.1 Identifying Your Unhealthy Helping and Giving Behaviors

Directions: Use the scale to rate the items for how well they describe you. Consult a friend, loved one, or therapist to assist if needed. You may answer with a specific person or relationship in mind, or in regards to your relationships in general. You may find it especially helpful to write down examples next to items you agree are true of you.

1=Strongly Disagree
2=Disagree
3=Neutral
4=Agree
5=Strongly Agree

Bearing Others' Negative Consequences

____1. I bail out others from their self-imposed troubles.

____2. My help softens the consequences of others' mistakes.

Taking Care of Things for Others They Should Do Themselves

____3. I do things for others that most people do for themselves, but they don't reciprocate.

____4. I provide things for others that most people of their age and abilities provide for themselves.

____5. I have one-sided relationships where I'm the giver and others are the takers.

Making or Accepting Bogus Explanations for Poor Performance or Undesirable Behavior

____6. I let others off the hook by accepting their questionable justifications for poor performance or bad behavior.

____7. I defend others when people question their behavior or lack of progress.

Covering for Others by Lying or Doing Their Work

____8. I lie to keep others from getting into trouble.

____9. I do others' work for them so they can do well and/or avoid trouble.

Overlooking Violated Boundaries and Agreements

____10. I let others get away with breaking our agreements.

____11. I don't follow through with threatened consequences.

Accommodating Others

____12. I make it easy for others not to change in needed ways.

____13. I cater to others' "manufactured needs" arising from a poorly managed mental or physical health condition or addiction.

____14. I'm the kind of person that caters to others' needs and wishes.

Impulsively Rescuing Others

_____15. I instantly offer help without thinking and later regret it.

_____16. I immediately intervene to solve others' problems even when my help isn't really needed or asked for.

_____17. I have relationships with people that are characterized by their crisis and my rescuing.

Over-helping/Over-giving

_____18. When it comes to family or work groups, I tend to do more than my share of the group's work.

_____19. I tend to be so generous in my relationships that I have trouble taking care of my needs.

_____20. I tend to give a lot in a relationship and then feel hurt that others don't give as much.

Compute an average by adding up all your responses and dividing by 20 (the closer your score to 5, the greater the problem). Look at the items you marked with a 3 or higher to identify your problem areas. What are your most typical unhealthy helping and giving behaviors and in which relationships do they occur?

The Twelve Red Flags of Unhealthy Helping and Giving

Once again, my intention isn't to suggest we act selfishly. It's good to be helpful and supportive to others. But there's a big difference between healthy and unhealthy helping and giving, and sometimes our helpful, generous intentions unexpectedly lead to unhealthy helping or giving. That's why it's important to know how to tell when your helping and giving have crossed the line from healthy to unhealthy.

Here are twelve red flags that signal you've crossed that line. When you see one or more of these, it's usually time to reconsider your helping and giving.

Red Flag 1: *It's obvious your help and giving fosters dependence, irresponsibility, incompetence, or poor character.* This is the number one sign it's time to back off. Healthy helping promotes other people's growth, independence, and the development of their positive potential. Unhealthy (dysfunctional) helping and giving does the opposite.

Red Flag 2: *The recipient has violated numerous agreements, required many bailouts, and hasn't used the help to do as promised.* When people use your help and giving to escape responsibility over and over again, it's time to recognize it's unhealthy.

Red Flag 3: *The help or giving helps someone to stagnate, or become stuck in an age-inappropriate, earlier stage of development, or prevents them from developing needed life or job skills.* You can be so helpful and giving that you assist in the creation of people that can't take care of themselves or do their jobs well. Unhealthy helping and giving can doom others to less than they're capable of. Healthy helping and giving empowers people. It promotes others' independence and life progress; it doesn't retard it.

Red Flag 4: *Your helping or giving requires your dishonesty or somehow compromises your integrity.* For example, making bogus excuses for another or covering for them, are rarely healthy. Although there are exceptions, such as when our dishonesty saves someone from becoming a victim of violence, healthy helping and giving rarely requires deception, secrets, or violation of laws, rules, or our moral code.

Red Flag 5: *You feel manipulated into helping or giving.* Manipulation is a bad sign. It warns of a potentially challenging situation with a person willing to push our helping and giving boundaries for their own selfish ends. Sometimes it signals a taker with a psychopathic or anti-social personality (the "takeriest" of all the takers).

Red Flag 6: *Your helping or giving is increasingly unsustainable given your emotional, physical, or material resources.* Although there are exceptions, typically, healthy helping and giving doesn't exceed your means.

Red Flag 7: *Instead of strengthening your relationship, your helping or giving weakens it.* Compared to healthy helping and giving, unhealthy helping and giving often creates relationship imbalance, conflict, hurt, and resentment.

Red Flag 8: *Your helpful accommodations make it easier for someone to remain physically unhealthy, put off getting professional help, avoid taking their medication or working their program, etc.* Healthy helping and giving empowers people to better manage their condition. It doesn't make it easy for people avoid sustainable solutions for sobriety or health.

Red Flag 9: *Your help or giving in a group setting leads others to slack.* Healthy helping and giving inspires a cooperative group culture where people help and give to one another and do their share.

Red Flag 10: *Your one-time, modest offer of help or giving has morphed into an unintended long-term obligation you resent or find burdensome.* Sometimes, one kind gesture can commit us to helping or giving more than we initially intended, leaving us feeling stuck in an unwanted situation.

Red Flag 11: *You're in a self-sacrificing relationship reeking of codependence.* It's one-sided and closeness is based on one person being a giver and the other a taker. Much of the love and intimacy in the relationship is experienced in the context of the one person's distress and the other's rescuing or enabling, or one person's excessive giving and the other's excessive taking.

Red Flag 12: *You're willing to overlook the ill effects of your helping and giving because it makes you feel or look like a "good" person.* It's not necessarily bad to feel like a good person because you're generous, helpful, or supportive. But it's a bad sign when that's the main point of your helping or giving and it leads you to overlook the damaging effects of your helping and giving.

Two

Unhealthy Helping and Giving Relationships

While I'm in this confession booth I call a book, I must admit to many relationships heavily based on my helping and giving, some of which might classify as codependent. There is, for example, my almost two-year college live-in relationship with Marco, a sometimes sober addict whose intelligence and artistic talent suggested great potential. At nineteen, I was wise beyond my years, but not wise enough. My hunger for love and approval and his proclamations of everlasting love led me to financially support him while I attended college full-time and worked thirty hours a week.

I readily accepted Marco's dependency and compensated for his dereliction of his adult duties. But Marco became a human python of bone-crushing love and dependence. I try to leave at least five times, usually after some episode where Marco was too controlling or did too many drugs or spent too much of the money I earned on something we didn't need. But each time I left, he fell apart. He threatened suicide and said no one would ever love me like he did (true, in its own warped way). His distress was downright heart breaking and my empathy led me to soften. To settle him down I agreed to come back.

However, my dissonance intensified as college graduation neared and Marco deteriorated. One night, he drops so much acid (LSD) I don't know if he's ever coming back to Earth. For almost 24 hours, he lies in the bathtub sputtering from some other dimension of time and space. What will happen next time? (And I am reasonably sure there will be a next time.) I find myself increasingly reluctant to commit to the possibility of taking care of a drug-fried Marco. I finally end the relationship.

Codependent relationships were only part of my dysfunctional giving arsenal. The help I provided to my teens and young adult children often teetered on the brink of enabling (my supportive efforts snatched from the jaws of unhealthy helping only through uncomfortable boundary setting). I've even enabled people to enable, participating in what I call in this chapter an *enabling chain*. I've also had *unhealthy dual helping relationships* where my giving led to having two different, and contradictory relationships with the same person at the same time. This chapter focuses on these common, but complicated, unhealthy helping and giving relationships.

Codependent Relationships

Although some people might call any dysfunctional helping or giving relationship codependent, I think of a codependent relationship as a specific type (and degree) of unhealthy giving relationship.

Codependent relationships are typically long term, close relationships with an extremely high degree of attachment and enmeshment between the giver and recipient, although some people have have relatively brief but intense codependent relationships. Although codependent relationships can exist between friends, and occasionally begin with helping someone that's practically a stranger, they're usually primary relationships such as parent-child relationships, or romantic and spousal-type relationships. Regardless, they're imbalanced relationships and for the most part, one-sided. The giver plays the role of extreme caregiver, rescuer, supporter, or confidante while the recipient (or taker) plays the role of patient, victim, or entitled royalty.

The most extreme codependent relationships involve a close relationship revolving around one person's poor functioning and another's enabling and rescuing. These are relationships built on one person's being a giver and the other an under-functioning taker. Much of the love and intimacy in the relationship is experienced in the context of the one person's distress and the other person's rescuing or enabling, or one person's giving and the other person's receiving. The giver shows love and caring by making sacrifices to respond to the manufactured needs of a difficult or under-functioning other. The giver often depends on the other's poor functioning to satisfy emotional needs such as the need to feel needed, and the need to keep the other close due to fears of abandonment (Chapter 5 discusses the emotional sources of unhealthy helping and giving).

The giver's emotional enmeshment with the taker leads them to keenly feel the other's struggles and to feel extreme boundary guilt at the thought of limiting their help. This emotional arousal motivates reducing the other's suffering (and their own) with repeated intervention and makes them quickly retreat from any limits they set (for more on this topic, see Chapter 4).

Codependency likely occurs on a continuum. In the worst cases, the line between the giver's self and the other person becomes so blurred that the giver loses sight of who they are outside of the self-other relationship. This may happen if, for some time, the other's poor functioning has dominated the giver's life and limited their other relationships and activities. They may feel adrift if the the taker moves towards independence or recovery and may struggle to redefine themselves and their life in light of the other's change. This is one reason why therapy is often recommended for the family members of recovering addicts and alcoholics.

In the codependent relationship the taker is often bound to the giver because the giver's lengthy aid has impeded their maturity, life skills, or confidence. Or they may be dependent on the giver's assistance because the giver's care has enabled their addiction, or poor mental or physical health. Takers may also depend on the codependent relationship to feel loved since their poor functioning brings them care and concern from the giver. This further reduces their motivation to change (more on this in Chapter 6).

The Parent-Child Relationship: High in Enabling and Codependence Potential

There's probably no relationship with greater enabling and codependent relationship potential than the parent-child relationship. Trying to support their children, parents sometimes enable their children's dependence, irresponsibility, or poor health. I know for me, supporting my son and stepchildren without enabling them was one of my greatest parenting challenges. I'm not alone. The parent-child relationship is a potential minefield of unhealthy helping and giving. Many parents struggle with when to help or give to their children, how much, and for how long.

As you'll learn in later chapters, parents' enabling of their children often stems from guilt over their past parenting mistakes. Fears of abandonment can also motivate parents' dysfunctional helping and giving. Some parents fear that without their children's dependence, they'll have little or no relationship with them (see Chapter 5 for more of this line of thinking). They build a codependent relationship with their child so their child won't ever leave them.

The parent-child relationship is also susceptible to enabling and codependence because for many people, the parent role is defined by self-sacrifice and other-centeredness. Good parents put their children's needs before their own, taking care of them financially and otherwise. They rescue their children from perilous situations and protect them from harm. They act to reduce their children's suffering. Providing help to our children (regardless of their age, why they need our help, and whether it strains our resources), feels consistent with being a good and loving parent.

The parent-child relationship is also initially characterized by the child's natural dependence on the parent and the parent's responsibility for most, if not all, of the child's needs. This feature of the parent-child relationship typically undergoes a change as childhood ends and adulthood begins. However, some parent-child relationships fail to make this transition, or make it only partially. They continue the dependency long past its natural expiration date because one or both of them isn't ready due to fear, codependency, addiction, untreated or poorly treated mental health or developmental disorders, or because the helping arrangement satisfies unconscious emotional needs. For some parents, this parental giving can last a lifetime. According to the American Association of Retired Persons (AARP), almost a quarter of people in their seventies provide financial support to their adult children. [7]

This failure to transition may be even more likely if the offspring has a chronic illness, physical or cognitive limitation, or addiction, because the parent may not trust them to properly care for themself. The parent may even promote continued dependency so they can monitor their condition and protect them from harm, which also reduces their own anxiety about their loved one's wellbeing. Sometimes they're worried that their child won't fare well in a world that has trouble making room for those that are very sensitive, or have medical conditions, physical or cognitive limitations, or addictions. So rather than support their child in fighting that fight, they protect them from having to fight it at all.

When parents enable their adult, young adult, emerging adult or adolescent children it often reduces their offspring's ability to function at an adult level (or the level they're capable of given any real limitations). It may also prevent their offspring from learning important life lessons. Box 2.1 illustrates this idea. It lists a variety of life competencies and the helpfully intended parental behaviors that may sabotage them (keeping in mind that these also may apply to other types of relationships, such as spouses or friends). This is an interesting list because it links some common parental behaviors to specific negative maturational consequences for children.

Box 2.1 Parental Help That Reduces Offspring Competencies

Note: **Important Life Skill appears in bold** and *Examples of Enabling and Rescuing Acts that Interfere with Developing or Demonstrating this Competency appear in italics)*

Providing financially for oneself

- *Giving them money or paying their expenses such that they don't have to provide for themselves*

Good money management

- *Bailing them out of financial jams resulting from their poor budgeting or excessive spending*

Self-feeding and self-cleaning

- *Preparing all or most of their meals, providing their groceries, doing their laundry, and cleaning up after them*

Taking responsibility for consequences of poor decision-making (so one can learn from mistakes)

- *Paying for/reducing the results of their mistakes or irresponsibility*

Taking care of one's own physical and mental health

- *Managing their mental or physical health condition for them*
- *Accommodating their unhealthy behaviors*

Effective and responsible problem-solving

- *Solving/fixing their problems*
- *Completing or mostly completing information searches and bureaucratic problem-solving tasks for them*

Being resilient (able to handle life's challenges without falling apart)

- *Rescuing as soon as the other shows distress*
- *Excessive comforting/soothing of the other when they're upset*

Perseverance in the face of setbacks

- *Taking over as soon as the other stumbles*

Parent-child unhealthy helping and giving relationships are also among the most resistant to change because the thought of withdrawing help leaves parents fraught with dissonance due to strong conflicting feelings and thoughts—some (like guilt or fear) telling them to keep helping and others (like rationality), telling them it's not in the best interest of their child. This means that the prospect of boundary setting leaves them riddled with bullet holes of ambivalence.

I know this first-hand. I was all about supporting the education and career development of my son and three stepchildren and my husband followed my lead. But this help wasn't always as helpful as intended. For example, in a misguided effort to support one of my teen stepsons, we advocated for his release from an addiction treatment center to prevent his mother from sending him to a remote lock-down facility. He moved in with us and was uncommitted to his recovery, leading to many battles before he elected to move in with his stepfather who placed few demands on him.

Later, when we thought he was doing better, money we gave for tuition was spent on drugs and jewelry. Although we were deeply concerned about him, his addiction overrode his good character and we thought it best to withdraw our financial support. We didn't want to enable his drug use by making it easier for him to maintain it. But his other parents were understandably concerned he might end up on the streets or in the criminal justice system if they didn't provide for him, bail him out, and cover for him. His drug abuse continued for five more years until a devastating addiction-related car accident jump-started his sobriety. (Still sober almost a decade later, he has a successful career and a lovely wife and family.)

We had other experiences where our children didn't comply with helping agreements. For example, one violated agreement was, "We'll pay for your rent as long as you're taking a full load of college classes, but otherwise we expect you to support yourself by working." Our student dropped all but one of his classes and didn't tell us for a couple of months. We then reminded him of the agreement and told him it was now up to him to pay his own bills. To his credit, he immediately went to work and became financially independent. After a few years of working and taking care of himself, he was ready to go back to school. (He went on to complete a college degree and land a well-paying job).

Our parenting practice was to withdraw our help once we realized an agreement was breeched. We felt it important to make the point that you should honor your contracts. We wanted to send a message that it's okay to accept help, but *not* okay to take advantage of others' generosity—there's a difference between a hand-up and a hand-out. We also tried to provide temporary help for career development that ended once milestones were reached and they could provide for themselves. Most importantly, we didn't want to enable our children's underachievement through help that kept them comfortable beyond their means, despite performing below their capabilities. Such help often *de*motivates and creates dependency. My husband's perspective was that if they wished, they could underperform on their own dime but it wasn't a good use of our resources.

To my husband, setting helping boundaries was a relatively simple matter: if they don't uphold the agreement, then assistance is terminated. But setting helping boundaries with my son and three stepchildren proved difficult for me. I did it though, after finding comfort and strength in the knowledge it was the right thing to do. Good parenting requires it because it gives our children a better chance at success. As loving parents we should provide support that promotes our children's growth or progress. But we aren't really helpful if our support enables dependence, irresponsibility, incompetence, or poor character. Not enabling your children is also more sustainable because it's less likely to deplete your limited emotional, physical, and financial resources. You can also go to your grave knowing that they can take care of themselves.

The moral of this particular story is to guard against continuing your child's dependency past its natural expiration date. When childhood ends and adulthood begins, your relationship should change. While it was once good parenting to manage your child's life and provide for their needs, it's now good parenting to back off, providing only that which helps your emerging adult transition into adulthood. It's truly the end of an era in the life of your relationship and a time for autonomy-oriented help that provides tools for independence, rather than dependency-oriented help that suggests they can't take care of themselves. It's a letting go time, a time to redefine ourselves and our parent role, a time to trust that they love us enough that we won't lose them when we stop the money, a time to trust them to figure it out, a time to accept that they might not live the way we want them to. It's a time to gently push our babies out of the comfy home nest and assure them they can fly.

Holding back from rescuing your adult and emerging adult children is usually advisable, except in rare circumstances. If you don't pull back and require they step up, you may prevent the development of normal adult competencies such as being financially independent and responsible, dealing with life's bureaucracies, attaining gainful employment, and cooking, shopping, and cleaning for oneself, as well as other responsible adult behaviors. And as hard as it may be for you to retreat, it's generally a good idea to let them assume their own adult responsibilities, even when you know a better way to accomplish them, or they choose not to live their lives as you think they should. Remind yourself that too much help communicates a lack of faith in them, which undermines their confidence and willingness to try. Any help you provide should promote their life progress, not their stagnation.

Parent-child dysfunctional helping and giving relationships can stubbornly persist because they're frequently driven by our emotional needs (a topic of later chapters). They're often fueled by empathy (a topic of Chapter 4), and nourished by occasional honeymoons where the offspring treats the giver well, isn't in crisis, or does what they're supposed to. For example, emerging adult and adult offspring takers may make brief efforts to comply with the giving agreement (like paying back part of the money owed) or may do something considerate (such as treating the giver well on their birthday). They may make a step towards greater maturity or independence. Parents feed on these occasional bones of hope like ravenous dogs. These sporadic positive acts and hopeful signs temporarily avert the parent's anger and resentment from reaching the critical mass needed to motivate consistent boundary setting and the termination of assistance.

When Children Enable Parents

Of course sometimes the situation is reversed and it's the child enabling a parent. For example, Oscar enabled his father (who had both a gambling and an alcohol addiction) by regularly bailing him out of jail, lending him money, and paying his bills.

An adult child's enabling of a parent is most likely when a parent is emotionally immature, has a personality disorder (such as borderline personality disorder or anti-social personality disorder), or suffers from some other untreated psychiatric disorder or addiction. Sometimes such parents plant and nurture the seeds of a codependent relationship by *parentifying* the child from an early age. The parent puts the child in a self-sacrificing caregiving role where they're expected to respond to their parent's emotional needs and assume many of their parent's responsibilities. Some children assume these responsibilities to be close to their under-functioning parent. The parent and child become enmeshed in an unhealthy relationship where their roles are reversed and the child takes care of their parent despite the high cost to their own personal development.

Julie's case provides a good example. Julie was the eldest child of Marie, a woman suffering from untreated bipolar disorder who abused prescription drugs and alcohol. Marie was divorced from Julie's father who remarried a much younger woman and started a new family. Julie saw him infrequently (partly because it upset Marie so much) although he supported the family financially.

From an early age, Julie made sure her younger brother was fed, bathed, and made it to school. By the time she was in seventh grade, Julie did the family's shopping, cleaning, and laundry. By all outside appearances, things were going fine, but only because Julie assumed her mother's adult responsibilities and both Julie and her brother covered for Marie by pretending to teachers, neighbors, and relatives that everything was good at home.

Of course Julie was just a child and didn't know she was enabling her mother. Her deep emotional connection to Marie compelled her to take care of Marie's responsibilities, especially since Marie frequently told her that she didn't know what she'd do without her, and referred to Julie as her angel and "Mommy's little helper." But Julie's help masked the depth of her mother's illness to people that may have compelled her to seek needed treatment. Meanwhile, Marie didn't feel the need to cultivate other relationships since she had the devoted Julie.

As Julie grew into a young woman and her mother's illness and alcoholism progressed, her mother's dependence interfered with Julie living the normal life of a person her age. Marie had tantrums if Julie left her alone for long, saying that Julie was a selfish, back-stabbing daughter (among other potty-mouthed epithets). When Julie was away, Marie called her incessantly until she returned. Julie became increasingly resentful that her mother's needs always took precedence, but when she talked of moving out, her mother grew despondent and threatened to kill herself.

Julie's ambivalence (and depression) deepened. She felt called to live her own life but feared her mother would commit suicide if she did. She struggled with feeling disloyal when she attempted to have a life independent of her mother. This went on for several more years. Then, with the help of a good therapist, Julie realized Marie was declining despite her loving care, and she was taking Julie down with her. Julie began setting boundaries, ignoring Marie's charge that she was a cold-hearted witch when she did. She expressed confidence in her mother's ability to get better. She accepted that if her mother chose not to accept professional help, this was her mother's choice, not her responsibility.

When Julie came home to find her mother swallowed a handful of pills because Julie was abandoning her, Julie didn't rescue by telling her mother what she wanted to hear and doing as she wished (which would have meant never having a life of her own). Instead, she calmly called 911, and then called her grandparents.

Marie's parents arrived the next day and Marie was admitted to a dual-diagnosis treatment program (one that treats both addiction and psychiatric disorders). In family therapy, Julie made it clear that she'd no longer enable Marie's drinking and poor management of her mental illness. She said a relationship was possible only if Marie worked to get healthy. Marie completed treatment and received good aftercare involving Alcoholics Anonymous, a psychiatrist, and a psychotherapist. Julie used what she learned in therapy to maintain healthy boundaries with her mother. Eventually, Marie and Julie forged a healthier mother-daughter relationship.

Unhealthy Dual Helping Relationships

Sometimes helping a friend or loved one involves a *dual relationship.* When it comes to helping others, dual relationships commonly arise when we try to help a friend or relative by lending them money, renting them a place to live, or hiring them to work for us. These helping actions create a situation where we have two potentially contradictory relationships with the same person: a business relationship and a personal relationship.

If they pay back the money as agreed, stick to the housing agreement, capably and reliably perform the job we hired them for, and use our help to move forward in their life, the dual helping relationship can work. But if they don't, *interrole conflict* occurs. The dual relationship becomes a dueling relationship as the demands of our business and personal roles clash. Honoring the demands of one role means going against what is called for by the other role. These clashing role demands create internal and interpersonal conflict.

Dual helping relationships are potentially risky and stressful. For example, as a lender, we typically have a formal contract and expect prompt payment. We feel it's appropriate to take action against borrowers that don't comply with the agreement. It's nothing personal, it's just business. However, if we're also the borrower's loved one or friend, we may struggle with asking for repayment, resent having to repeatedly beg for it, and seethe over their spending when they should pay us back.

The same goes for helping your friend or relative by becoming their landlord. If a tenant-stranger failed to pay their rent or perform agreed-upon duties, as landlord you probably wouldn't hesitate to speak up or kick them out. But boundary setting is complicated when you're also the tenant's close relative or friend. It can feel petty, selfish, mean, and dissonant with our role as supportive family member or friend.

Trying to help a friend or relative by hiring them to work for you is also risky. If an employee takes long lunches or leaves early, slacks, or performs poorly in some regard, as an employer, you'd normally do something like call them out, give them a warning, write them up, or fire them. But if the employee and you have a dual relationship, you'll likely struggle with saying or doing something about their poor job performance.

The emotional fallout from a failed dual helping relationship can be great. When people close to you break agreements and take advantage of your generosity, it's hurtful and disappointing. Who is this selfish person willing to take advantage of you and harm your relationship? This isn't the person you respect and agreed to help! When you go out on a limb to help, you don't expect the other person to cut off the branch and leave you hanging. If only they lived up to the agreement there'd be no problem. Now instead of your help making you the good guy as you intended, you become the bad guy when you try to enforce the agreement.

Meanwhile, they feel betrayed if you treat the relationship as a business relationship and don't cut them the slack they desire and expect if you are truly a loving relative or friend. In their minds, they aren't just anybody and your treating them as you would an employee, renter, or borrower, is hurtful. Conflicts over the business relationship erode trust and damage the personal relationship, sometimes temporarily, sometimes permanently.

Unhealthy dual relationships create dissonance and ambivalence. The resulting anger, resentment, disappointment, frustration, and conflict can erode a once decent relationship. You should probably think long and hard and then some more before entering into a dual relationship, especially if the other person has a history of breaking agreements and taking advantage of your or other people's help. However, because people with such histories certainly can change and may need a helping hand and second chance, it's sometimes worth the risk.

Does this mean you shouldn't help friends or relatives by lending them money, renting them a place to live, or giving them a job? Not necessarily. As the Beatles once said, "We all get by with a little help from our friends." Dual helping relationships sometimes work well. But if I were you, I'd avoid dual helping relationships with people who have:

- Failed to honor past agreements (including those with other friends, families, landlords, exes, the courts, etc.)
- Demonstrated a tendency to take advantage of your or other people's helpfulness or generosity
- Difficulty using alcohol or drugs responsibly
- A track record of resisting or rebelling against authority
- Exhibited signs of narcissism (e.g., feel entitled, have little empathy, blame others for their problems, are arrogant)

These dual relationships are high-risk and unlikely to work out. And, while people with codependent tendencies often ignore these risk factors and repeatedly enter into risky dual helping relationships, codependence isn't necessary for an unexpectedly stressful dual helping relationship.

So, my advice: if you choose to enter into a dual helping relationship, go in with your eyes open, knowing it's a risk and able to take a loss if you have to. But be aware that money isn't the only thing at stake. There are emotional and relationship risks as well, so consider the above risk factors before offering this type of help. If you choose to go ahead, set clear ground rules, including expectations regarding repayment, work performance, or rent, how long you're willing to help, etc., ideally in writing. Also, be prepared to call the deal off if:

- They choose not to honor the agreement
- They use your assistance to avoid the hard work of being a mature adult instead of using it as a springboard to self-reliance
- You're becoming resentful, or feel disrespected and taken advantage of
- It's hurting your relationship
- You can no longer afford it

See Chapter 9 for help with ending helping and giving arrangements.

Unhealthy Helping and Giving Relationships with Difficult Takers

It's easy to blame the giver for the mess they're in. They certainly bear some responsibility for promoting the dysfunctional helping and giving relationship. They have the power to change their behavior and to change the relationship dynamic. Without their cooperation, the unhealthy situation would burn out like a fire starved for oxygen. But let's face it, some people make it especially difficult to set limits on our helping or giving. These difficult takers assume a variety of forms, but in general they're manipulative, selfish, entitled, and immature (and occasionally, dangerous).

If taking were an Olympic sport, the difficult taker would get a medal. Some play the part of the perpetual, pitiful victim. They play on our empathy to convince us they're casualties of unjust circumstance and worthy and deserving of our aid. Some selfish takers stubbornly refuse to take care of themselves knowing from past experience that the people that care about them will feel compelled to take care of things for them.

Some difficult takers deliberately wait the giver out, knowing that the giver will eventually assume responsibility for their personal tasks. These privileged, entitled takers find responsibility too hard, tiresome, or restrictive and seek to pawn it off on others for as long as they can get away with it. They have little empathy for the giver and feel little or no guilt as their personal giver toils on their behalf.

Unresolved emotional issues, such as they didn't receive care at an important time in their life, make some difficult takers seek the care of others. They may want care from a particular person, usually a parent, because they want proof of that person's love or want that person to atone for some real or imagined sin against them. These people stubbornly cling to their dependence as they try to get these emotional needs met.

Drugs and alcohol abuse are used by some difficult takers to manufacture a need for help, but addiction also fuels desperation for the resources to fuel their habit. Addiction seems to turn some people into difficult takers that are needy, demanding, and persistent in the face of a giver's boundaries.

Likewise, there are difficult takers needing help due to poor management of their mental or physical illness or disability. For example, they don't take medications as prescribed, take poor care of themselves, and don't comply with recommendations from health professionals. As a result, their physical or emotional fragility leads to their dependence on other people. Because we care about them and believe they can't or won't engage in better self-care, we respond to their self-manufactured needs. In such cases, givers often feel their actions are about risk-reduction. They believe they're the only thing standing between the taker and certain disaster so they have to help or give. Sometimes that's true but sometimes it's not. Admittedly, it can be challenging to determine whether our help is risk-reduction or enabling. I recommend gathering as much data as you can to accurately access the situation. I wouldn't be too quick to conclude someone's not up to the task of sobriety or good mental or physical health (more on this later).

Sometimes the taker's continued dependence on the giver arises from their personality. Some difficult takers are, to put it in bald psychological terms, personality disordered. Let's put it this way, they have a stable constellation of personality traits that consistently leads to problems in their relationships and to unhealthy ways of getting their needs met. Some may even fit the criteria for "official" personality disorders defined in the *Diagnostic and Statistical Manual of Mental Disorders (DSM)*, such as:

- Anti-social personality disorder (tends to act impulsively, has little regard for others, deceitful, has an exaggerated sense of self-importance)
- Borderline personality disorder (requires others to soothe them, tends to feel victimized, has extreme emotions, tends to see problems as catastrophes)
- Personality disorders involving narcissist traits (feels entitled, has little empathy, blames others for their problems, arrogant). [8] [9]

The personality traits of unhealthy givers and takers are discussed in more detail in Chapter 4.

People that have extreme anti-social and narcissistic traits are sometimes called psychopaths and they're some of the most difficult of all the takers. They may not be truly evil, but they will intentionally scheme, lie, and manipulate people into helping or giving to them. They lead us to believe their need is greater than it is, or that they're hapless victims of circumstance deserving of help (which is usually far from the truth). Many malinger by fabricating physical or emotional problems, attributing their lack of initiative or troubles to false causes, or intentionally doing things to create or exaggerate physical or psychological problems. These takers manipulate. They con us into helping and giving to them, and bully us when we try to set boundaries with them.

Lacking empathy for others, anti-social and narcissistic takers don't much care about how their demands affect the giver. They just want what they want and prefer that others assume the cost. Believing they're superior and deserving of others' rewards, they sometimes blame their taking on the giver's stupidity or naiveté. These extreme takers are often like parasites that move from one host to another. Once the giver finally sets boundaries or is sucked dry, they move on to their next kind-hearted victim. In my opinion, these takers are the craftiest and cruelest of them all because they so willingly take advantage of others' kindness and generosity, and don't feel that badly about it.

If you're waiting around for a difficult taker to change so that you won't have to do the hard work of boundary-setting, you could wait forever, especially if they're addicted or personality disordered and your giving enables their poor functioning and dependency. To avert the many negative consequences of unhealthy helping and giving discussed in the next chapter, it's likely you'll have to set boundaries, and in many cases, eventually end the relationship. Chapter 9 on assertive boundary setting may help. But, as the old American adage goes, an ounce of prevention is worth a pound of cure. Do your best to avoid entering into relationships with difficult takers and when one sneaks past you, get out, or set boundaries at the first signs of trouble.

Enabling Chains

Unhealthy helping relationships are sometimes part of a chain of interdependent helping and giving relationships I call an enabling chain. For example, because of his regular bailouts to his girlfriend Mariah, Dylan often borrowed money from family members to make his bills. The reason Mariah borrowed money from Dylan was because she gave a lot of her money to her mother. Her mother needed it because she was supporting Mariah's adult brother and sister (who, by the way, were technically capable of supporting themselves). So, Dylan's family members enabled his enabling of Mariah, and Dylan's enabling of Mariah enabled her to enable her sister and mother and her mother's enabling of her son and daughter!

The enabling chain consists of multiple, linked enabling relationships involving at least three people: the taker, the primary unhealthy giver, and an accessory giver. The accessory giver is a loyal friend, relative, or partner that aids and abets the primary giver's enabling of the taker (essentially enabling the enabler). For example, when a giver's assistance to another leads to financial hardship, their accessory helper may lend them money, pay for things, offer moneymaking opportunities, or provide other material support in the form of generous gifts—help they wouldn't need if not for their dysfunctional giving. Givers sometimes have an "enabling support system" where their unhealthy helping and giving is sustained by multiple accessory givers. [10] [11]

Box 2.2 helps you decide whether you're part of an enabling chain.

Box 2.2 Are You Part of an Enabling Chain?

Consider the following questions to determine whether you're part of an enabling chain.

1. Does your friend or loved one need your help because they're giving their resources to a taker(s) that wouldn't need help if they were more responsible for taking care of themselves?
2. Does your help make it possible for someone to continue to enable other people?
3. Do you require the resources of others due to your dysfunctional helping or giving? Do you rely on people close to you to provide emotional, material, or financial support needed because of your unhealthy helping and giving? Who might be enabling your enabling?
4. Do you have an enabling support system?
5. Should you consider helping within your means so that you don't have to depend on others to support your unhealthy helping and giving habit?

If you're the primary giver, you can break the chain by only helping and giving within your true means (instead of depending on other people's help so that you can enable someone else). For example, let's say you now only help if you can truly afford to and if it doesn't compromise your self-sufficiency. And of course, you can break the chain by not enabling the other and therefore eliminating the need for your accessory giver(s).

Accessory helpers sometimes break the chain once they realize that their help indirectly enables another they believe is undeserving, lazy, or manipulative and has hurt the primary giver whom they care about. Sometimes the taker breaks the chain. For example, they may break the enabling link between themselves and their primary giver by getting sober. They also may grow more mature and accept their adult responsibilities, or become embarrassed by their dependence and motivated to achieve self-sufficiency.

Helping and Giving Entrapment

Most people find themselves entrapped in an uncomfortable helping or giving situation at some point in their lives. They make what they intend to be a one-time or short-term modest offer of help or giving only to find themselves in an unintended long-term obligation that's hard to get out of. I call this *helping and giving entrapment.*

The psychological forces of commitment and consistency partly explain helping and giving entrapment. Consistency is socially valued and simply acting consistently with our past actions saves time and thinking. So once we help or give, we can easily find ourselves automatically agreeing to do it again. People find it harder to say no when they've already said yes. Let your neighbor borrow something once and it'll be hard to say no when they ask again. Help someone out by giving them a ride home from work one time and you may find yourself doing it every night. It's akin to what psychologists call the *foot-in-the-door effect,* where a small commitment gradually gives rise to larger, related commitments.

The ways we justify our helping and giving also promote entrapment. Many unhealthy givers impulsively give, help, or rescue and then justify why it was the right thing for to do. But once we justify why we should help or give (or continue to help or give), these justifications pave the way for more of the same and escalate our commitment. It can feel hypocritical to stop and inconsistent with our own stated reasons for why we must help or give. After all, continuing to help or give is consistent with our own past actions and justifications.

Helping entrapment is particularly likely when we're heavily invested in fixing or helping someone. In psychology, the entrapment concept includes the idea that people escalate their commitment to a losing course of action to justify their prior commitment. Basically, when their intervention is costly yet ineffective, people often invest even more. They don't want to lose what they've invested and they don't want to deal with feeling foolish about their now-apparent poor decision to intervene, so they keep trying to make it work. Cognitive psychologists call this the *sunk cost fallacy* and explain that in decision making, humans are often more concerned about what they might lose than they are about what they might gain. Social psychologists explain that it's related to *dissonance due to effort*, which arises when we freely chose to sacrifice for something or someone and it turns out it wasn't worth it. To avoid feeling like a fool for giving so much to a losing cause, we try to convince ourselves our assistance wasn't a mistake. Unfortunately, these rationalizations further cement our commitment to the unhealthy giving.

Think about this way: When we heavily invest time, energy, and resources into making something work, it's hard to walk away with nothing to show for it. Terminating our giving means losing our investment (e.g., effort, time, hope, money) and accepting that our giving had a poor outcome. It requires confronting our feelings of foolishness for committing our resources to a losing course of action. Some people hold on to an unhealthy helping and giving relationship just to avoid facing the uncomfortable fact that their giving was a mistake and their efforts and resources were wasted. Of course the longer they give and the more resources they commit, the harder it becomes to back away, since what they lose becomes greater the longer they stay.

When our help creates dependence and incompetence and we believe withdrawing our help will cause hardship to the other, helping entrapment may be even more pronounced due to deep ambivalence (later in the book I'll talk more about this *boundary guilt*). We may feel that we have no choice but to continue even when we don't want to. It can feel mean, rude, or petty to tell someone we no longer wish to share our resources with them. These boundary-setting barriers will be considered in more detail later. In the meantime, reading the next chapter on the negative consequences of unhealthy helping and giving may weaken the bonds of helping entrapment.

There are many other reasons why we may feel trapped in an unhealthy helping and giving situation. These include not knowing how to have an effective boundary-setting conversation. Lacking assertiveness skills, some people become entrapped in a helping and giving situation simply because they don't know how to say no to requests, or how to set boundaries with people that take advantage of their kindness and generosity. Box 2.3 helps you challenge your helping entrapment and Chapter 9 on healthy helping boundary skills helps with the assertiveness skills needed to set healthy helping and giving boundaries.

Box 2.3 Challenging Helping and Giving Entrapment

1. Do you feel trapped in a helping arrangement that's required much more from you than you expected when you first agreed to help?
2. What did you think you were signing up for when you offered help or agreed to give?
3. Would you have agreed if you knew it meant a long-term commitment with these costs?
4. If you're providing more help than you intended (and with negative outcomes), must you continue to honor your past commitment to helping? Is it time to cut your losses?

Three

The Negative Consequences of Unhealthy Helping and Giving

I don't call it unhealthy helping and giving for nothing. It's full of good intentions gone badly, unexpectedly causing harm to others, our relationships, and us. Sad as it is, bending over backwards to help or give to others can sometimes break both your back and your heart, and not be nearly as helpful as you intended.

Previous chapters touched on some of the negative consequences of unhealthy helping but this chapter explains in more detail just why unhealthy helping and giving are so problematic. Understanding these potential harms is important. It makes it easier to recognize when a helping or giving situation is out of hand, and can motivate us to set and maintain healthy helping boundaries even when it's uncomfortable. This chapter examines how unhealthy helping and giving harms givers and recipients, as well as relationships, and groups.

Harms To Givers

Giving can push the limits of our emotional, physical, and financial resources and it can create stressful relationship complications (these are discussed later in the chapter). The burden of helping and giving is made heavier by the fact that many givers are alone in their caring, without much support from others.

Givers in long-term relationships with difficult takers suffer more than other givers. Emotionally speaking, they're more likely to experience feelings of resentment, hurt, and victimization. It's hurtful when others don't appreciate the sacrifices made on their behalf, or when they act entitled to our help or resources, oblivious or uncaring about the impact on us (especially an issue if we're chronically ill or an elder). When givers repeatedly sacrifice time, energy, or money that wouldn't be necessary if others only did what they should, givers often become resentful—especially if providing help means they have difficulty meeting their own responsibilities or taking care of themselves. Givers can feel entrapped and victimized by manipulative others that refuse to get it together.

Stress, worry, and anxiety plague some unhealthy givers, especially those in codependent relationships. Distressing internal conflict (cognitive dissonance) may arise due to contradictory thoughts such as, "I can't do this anymore but I don't see how I can stop" and "I want to set boundaries but I'll feel selfish if I do." Some givers obsess about troubled others and what else they can do to engineer their change or solve their problems. They worry about dwindling resources and what will happen if they no longer help. They fret over why the other makes so little progress despite their best efforts to provide resources, information, or support.

If the taker is disrespectful, selfish, and achieves little despite their potential, givers feel sad and hurt. When the taker makes a step towards independence, maturity, or health only to falter and go backwards, givers experience disappointment. They feel stressed when their helping and giving strains their resources and overloads them with extra work, and when their helping and giving lead to relationship strain or conflict. Some givers become so stressed, anxious, and depressed they self-medicate with drugs or alcohol. [12]

Stress taxes our bodies and long-term stress from unhealthy helping and giving can have negative physical effects. Indeed, some research suggests that interpersonal stressors (those arising from our relationships and interactions with others), are the most upsetting and long-lasting in impact.

People with preexisting medical conditions may find that stress and hurt from unhealthy helping and giving relationships aggravates their condition.

For these people, physical health is a delicate balance easily thrown off-kilter by stress. Stress is hard on our bodies but it's even worse for the already compromised or struggling body systems of people with chronic medical conditions like diabetes, cancer, HIV/AIDS, COPD, and autoimmune diseases such as lupus or multiple sclerosis.

People under stress for extended periods often get sick. Scientists in the field of psychoneuroimmunology (PNI) report that immune cell activity is disrupted by the adrenaline and other hormones released when we're stressed. To aggravate the situation, when stressed, many people don't sleep well and don't practice good *self-care.* They don't eat right or exercise enough, and some self-medicate with alcohol or other drugs. This further weakens their bodies and diminishes their ability to effectively cope and recover.

Carrying other people's burdens may become too much to bear. A persistent pattern of unhealthy helping or giving can lead to *burnout,* a state of emotional, physical, and mental exhaustion. Burnout is a common result of long-term involvement in emotionally demanding situations. People with burnout frequently exhibit such symptoms as negativity and irritability. They experience stress-induced medical problems like gastrointestinal problems, and physical symptoms (somatic symptoms) such as headaches, that are reflections of emotional stress. Decreased cognitive functioning is another potential consequence of burnout. People suffering from burnout sometimes have trouble processing information as well as they once did and experience memory problems. According to research, a giver is more likely to experience burnout when they're highly emotionally involved without adequate social support, and see few positive results from their helping.

Compassion fatigue is a type of caregiver burnout that arises when continually bearing witness to the suffering of others traumatizes us. Trauma from continually empathizing with the suffering of others is called *secondary trauma.* When we're empathic, continually bearing witness to the suffering of others can result in secondary trauma and compassion fatigue. Compassion fatigue is probably greatest when a helper has a personal history of trauma, lacks social support, and has trouble coping with the demands of caregiving. [13] [14]

Unhealthy givers sometimes reach a point where their financial, mental, or physical health is jeopardized by their generosity and care for others. Box 3.1 assists you in identifying some of the negative personal effects of your giving.

Box 3.1 How Are You Negatively Affected By Your Helping and Giving?

Use the scale to rate the items, using "NA" for non-applicable if an item doesn't apply to you. Consult a friend, loved one, or therapist to assist if needed. You may answer with a specific person or relationship in mind, or in regards to your relationships in general.

1=Strongly Disagree
2=Disagree
3=Neutral
4=Agree
5=Strongly Agree

____1. I resent having to sacrifice because other people aren't doing what they should.
____2. I resent that my helping and giving means I have fewer resources.
____3. I resent that my helping and giving means I have less time.
____4. I resent that the burden of help seems to fall all on me.
____5. Due to the helping situation, I experience worry, fear, and dread.
____6. I'm disappointed that despite my best efforts to help others move forward, they have made little progress.
____7. I feel disappointed that my helping didn't have the results I intended.
____8. After all I have done for others, I'm hurt that they don't treat me better.
____9. I'm hurt by the fact that I have done so much to help others yet they do not seem to fully appreciate it.

_____10. I'm hurt that low-functioning others aren't motivated to change after seeing what taking care of them is doing to me.
_____11. I feel angry that the person I have helped so much has broken their promises to better take care of themselves or their responsibilities.
_____12. I feel angry because they don't stick to the agreements or bargains we made in exchange for my help.
_____13. I feel angry that others take advantage of my giving.
_____14. I feel hopeless and depressed.
_____15. I'm an "emotional wreck" due to my efforts to help another.
_____16. My helping and giving have negatively affected my physical health.
_____17. I find myself using more drugs or alcohol to manage the stress from giving to and helping others.
_____18. Because of my giving, I have not been taking care of myself as well as I should.
_____19. To avoid embarrassment, I don't always tell people when I help or give.
_____20. I am embarrassed that others remain so dependent on me.
_____21. I have lost a lot of sleep because of the helping situation.
_____22. I am extremely stressed because of the helping situation.
_____23. I have financial stress as a result of my helping and giving.
_____24. I feel overworked as a result of my helping and giving.
_____25. I feel frustrated by the helping situation.

Compute an average by adding up all your responses and dividing by the number of items you rated (an average over 4 is of greater concern than one under 3). Reflect on your responses, paying special attention to items you marked with a 4 or a 5. What does this tell you about the personal effects of your helping and giving? Are there other ways you're hurt, resentful, disappointed, frustrated, angry, or embarrassed? How else has your helping and giving affected your physical and mental health?

Harms To Recipients

Unhealthy helping and giving may hurt our emotional, physical, and financial health but there are also potential costs to the people we assist.

The two preceding chapters explained how things like absorbing the negative consequences of another's choices or excusing their irresponsible behavior, prevent people from progressing in their lives. You also read how our giving can compromise another's self-sufficiency and independence when they fail to develop normal age-appropriate competencies such as being financially responsible, taking care of their own basic needs for food and shelter, managing their emotions, dealing with life's bureaucracies, doing their share of the work, taking their share of responsibility, and cleaning up after themselves.

Remember too, that if our intervention repeatedly buffers another from experiencing unpleasant life experiences and their consequences, they may not develop the resilience and emotional maturity needed to effectively cope with the typical stresses and challenges of life. If your tendency is to rescue your children too quickly, they might not learn how to manage the uncomfortable emotions that come with stressful situations and imperfect decision-making. The ability to self-sooth and self-regulate our negative emotions are useful skills (and hallmarks of maturity) that help carry us through difficult times and setbacks, but they take practice to develop.

Our excessive rescuing can contribute to others' passivity and victimhood in the face of personal crisis. They don't learn that they can successfully handle or weather the frustrations and upset that come with difficult situations. This leads them to become easily overwhelmed and unglued in stressful circumstances, and sets us up for more rescuing. Givers sometimes set this self-perpetuating dysfunctional helping cycle in motion through their own fear and pessimism. Their fears that the other person can't handle the pains of life or that they aren't up to the tasks of independence leads to repeated intervention that prevents the other from developing needed life skills, including strength and persistence in the face of hardship.

Doing things for people that they should do for themselves may prevent them from being (or becoming) mature, self-reliant fully functioning adults that feel good about themselves in this world. That's because feeling competent is good for self-esteem. Ongoing intervention implies to the recipient that the giver believes they're incompetent or incapable. The giver's apparent lack of confidence in the recipient erodes their self-confidence as they see themselves through the giver's eyes. This, combined with a lack of life skills (aggravated by the giver's repeated intervention), reduces their confidence that they will be successful should they try (and if they don't believe they can "do it," they won't even bother trying). In essence, our helping can reduce what psychologists call *self-efficacy*. Self-efficacy, as noted by Albert Bandura, one of the leading psychologists of the last century, is critical to motivation and action. [15]

As discussed previously, there are also times when our help can enable addiction, or poor mental or physical health. For example, Rick paid the charges when his drug-addicted son Michael wrote bad checks all over town, and then declined to press charges when Michael stole his checks and forged his signature. He didn't want Michael to get in trouble with the law. Unfortunately, Rick's loving intervention prolonged Michael's drug abuse. Had he been prosecuted for this first-time offense, he would have been ordered by the court into a drug treatment program.

Accommodating behaviors also enable when they sand down the rough edges of another's suffering just enough that they can live with the now-modulated effects of their problem. And that reduces their motivation to seek a more independent, sustainable solution. While our ongoing support appears to be the answer to the problems generated by poorly treated illness or addiction, it's usually a temporary solution to the wrong problem. This is unfortunate when another's well being would be better served by working a behavior change program and complying with recommendations from medical and mental health professionals.

Take the case of Lisa who served as a 24/7 mental health hotline for her friend Natasha. Natasha called Lisa almost every day crying that she was ugly, no good, and that no one would ever love her. Lisa was usually able to calm and reassure Natasha only to find herself the next day listening to the same fears and insecurities and patching her up once again. Lisa also frequently dropped everything to stay with Natasha if she thought that Natasha might be in danger of harming herself. Unfortunately, these accommodations of Natasha's condition, although generous and well intentioned, prevented Natasha from getting the professional help she really needed, and interfered with Natasha learning how to manage her own mental health.

You can still help your friend or loved one, but ideally your help should empower them to enact sustainable solutions. You can, for instance, offer to help them identify community resources and professionals for expert support, diagnosis, and treatment. You can show a willingness to drive them to 12-step meetings or accompany them to appointments with mental health or medical professionals. You can provide emotional support as they navigate the maze towards better health and learn how to manage themselves and their situation. This, however, is quite different than providing help that enables them.

Altering our suspected enabling behaviors is usually worth a try because it sometimes benefits the other's maturity or health. We also benefit since we regain energetic and material resources. We also regain hope. But admittedly, changing our helping and giving won't always produce the results we want. We can offer help that supports healthy change but that doesn't mean they'll take us up on it. And honestly, stopping our enabling doesn't always jump-start the recipient's change. Fact is, some friends or loved ones in the throes of addiction or illness simply won't do what's needed to become healthy, regardless of what we do. In these extreme cases, you might provide help that reduces the life-threatening harms caused by their unhealthy behaviors so there's hope for their survival and future recovery. This *risk-reduction* or *harm-reduction* isn't the same thing as enabling.

Box 3.2 helps you think about the negative effects of your giving on the recipients.

Box 3.2 How Has Your Giving Negatively Impacted the Recipient?

Think about the unhealthy giving situation you're in. Consider how your help has affected the person you assisted and use the scale to rate the items.

1=Strongly Disagree
2=Disagree
3=Neutral
4=Agree
5=Strongly Agree

My help or giving has:

_____1. Enabled their irresponsibility by protecting them from the normal consequences of irresponsible choices and actions

_____2. Enabled their incompetence because they haven't had to learn or perfect important skills

_____3. Interfered with their independence because it has fostered dependence on me

_____4. Interfered with their confidence by not giving them a chance to try, fail, learn, persist, and succeed

_____5. Interfered with their confidence because it suggests that I think they're incompetent

_____6. Enabled their poor physical health by making it easier for them to continue poor health practices

_____7. Enabled their poor mental health by making it easy for them to put off seeking mental health care, or doing what they need to do to be well

_____8. Enabled their addiction or compulsion, making it easier for them to "feed it" and protecting them from its full consequences

_____9. Reduced their social skills (i.e., their ability to effectively communicate and interact with people) by making it easy for them not to interact with people

_____10. Interfered with their ability to manage their own emotions because they haven't had to learn how to self-calm or manage reactions to stressful situations

Additional negative consequences to the recipient not listed above:

Reflect on your responses, paying special attention to items you marked with a 4 or a 5. How can you change the support you provide so that it's more likely to truly helpful?

Harms To Giver-Recipient Relationships

Like many giving people, I was surprised when my helpful efforts led to relationship complications. I expected appreciation, liking, and respect for my competence and giving since I made others' lives easier with my generous assistance, and I helped solve others' problems. But sometimes, after a short honeymoon, I found myself feeling unappreciated, disrespected, and even disliked by the very people I helped and supported! What a surprising turn of events! Unfortunately, instead of bringing wanted social approval and closeness to others, excessive giving and helping can unexpectedly backfire. Social-psychological theory and research explains why.

One big reason is that unhealthy giving relationships often suffer from long-term inequity and long-term inequity reduces relationship satisfaction and increases relationship conflict. Relationship complications are likely when there's an ongoing relationship imbalance unjustified by age, developmental stage, or ability. Most people that give far more to their relationship partner than they receive eventually feel hurt, angry and resentful. Tension and conflict follow. This is especially likely if the giver expected their giving to be temporary and it turned out to be long-term, the taker isn't progressing, and the taker acts entitled and unappreciative.

Equity theory suggests that in relationships, people desire fairness in regards to what they put into a relationship and what they get out of it, and what the other person puts into it and gets out of it. [16] When one person gets more out of the relationship relative to the other, there's inequity. According to the theory, this imbalance leads to discomfort (guilt on the part of the person who is over-benefitting and resentment or anger on the part of the person that's under-benefitting). This relationship imbalance motivates people to do something so equity is restored.

Equity theory predicts that the overpaid person who is disproportionately benefitting (the recipient or taker) will act to restore balance by doing such things as contributing more to the relationship, taking less, or skewing their perceptions to minimize the inequity. Conversely, the underpaid person (the giver or helper) can reduce feelings of inequity by contributing less, increasing what they get out of the relationship, or skewing their perceptions to minimize the inequity.

The perceptual route to relationship equity restoration is usually favored by the taker, especially difficult takers—they restore balance by putting down the giver, minimizing the giver's efforts, and over-emphasizing anything they've done for the giver. This allows them to continue to accept the giving with little guilt and without having to increase what they put into the relationship.

Most givers also try a perceptual response to the inequity. They try to ignore or minimize the inequity to reduce their dissonance. For example, they may insist that the other will pay them back and equity will be restored, forget how much they've invested in helping the other, or exaggerate what the other has done in return. Some will repeatedly remind themselves they didn't help to get something in return so it doesn't matter if their help is unappreciated or unreciprocated. This can work for a while.

When changing their perceptions fails to settle them, givers usually act to restore balance by trying to increase their outcomes or trying to get the taker to increase their inputs. For example, if you're the giver, you may try to get the taker to appreciate you (by playing the martyr), pressuring them to do what you think they should (by nagging), or demanding they do things for you (by guilting them). Of course, another way for you to restore balance is to do less for the other person. But this usually happens only after other strategies for restoring equity have failed.

In the worst-case scenarios, relationship conflict brews as the giver becomes invasive, controlling, and whiny as they seek to restore relationship balance. For example, imagine the frustrated and angry parent giver who wants to see a return on their investment and so demands progress reports, asks invasive questions, pesters the other about how they're running their life, and tries to micro-manage the other's affairs.

While the giver may be rightly alarmed by the ongoing, imbalanced relationship and their wasted investment in the other, the nagging, controlling, shaming, and guilting used by some givers to get more out of the taker and restore equity, may come off as critical, demeaning, or condescending. Takers may respond with defensiveness and resistance. They may attack the giver who typically responds defensively and counter-counterattacks, the taker counter-counter-attacking and so on. The conflict escalates with each unpleasant verbal exchange (what social psychologists call *conflict spiraling*).

Like many givers, it sometimes takes me quite a while to reach a point where relationship inequity bothers me. I'm happy to share what I have with those that have less and it's okay if things aren't perfectly equal. I'm kind of a service-oriented person. I prefer giving more than taking. Being this way, I'm often surprised by those that take and take. I don't feel entitled to the fruits of others' labors and I'm uncomfortable receiving much from others without reciprocating. But clearly, not everyone is like me.

An elaboration of equity theory called the *equity sensitivity construct* suggests I'm a "Benevolent" and people comfortable with taking more than they receive are "Entitleds."[17] The equity sensitivity construct postulates that individuals fall along an "equity spectrum." At the one end of the spectrum are the Benevolents who contribute more to the relationship and are comfortable with putting in more than they get out; they put relationships before outcomes. I suspect that many unhealthy givers are Benevolents. At the other end are the Entitleds who are focused more on what they can get for the fewest inputs; they're not only comfortable with relationships where they get more than they put in, but they put outcomes first, and relationships second. I daresay that many difficult takers are entitleds. In the middle of the continuum are the Equity Sensitives preferring a balanced relationship where the input/outcome ratio of relationship partners is the same. Perhaps these equity-sensitive individuals are less prone to unhealthy helping and giving relationships and act more quickly to terminate them.

Nadler and Fisher's *threat to self-esteem model of helping* provides more insight into why our helping and giving doesn't always cast a warm, fuzzy glow over our relationships.[18] This model suggests that negative reactions to our giving are especially likely under four conditions. I've expanded and applied these to our topic of unhealthy helping and giving.

Condition 1: *The recipient feels the help or gift somehow implies they're inferior, incompetent, or lower in status than the giver. That's hard on their self-esteem or feels insulting.*

Sometimes being in a position to help or give highlights the giver's competence or success. That makes the recipient feel incompetent, unsuccessful, or lower in status in comparison. For example, you may want to help people you care about by generously sharing your good fortune with them, but to some, this is a reminder that they're less successful or less competent than you. Some people will even think you're doing it to rub their noses in your success and their failure. They then become defensive and motivated to take you down a few notches, or at the very least, they act ungratefully because they need to minimize the gifts or the giver to protect their ego.

Unsolicited help (assumptive help), including unsolicited advice, can also result in unexpected negative reactions, like defensiveness. If you're an extremely competent giver that jumps in and takes over others' tasks, often performing them more efficiently and effectively than others could've or would've, your unsolicited over-helping or rescuing can lead others feel judged or insulted. Likewise, your unsolicited advice may be misperceived as evidence that you think they're incompetent and higher in status than them. [19]

Condition 2: *The recipient believes they can't easily repay the debt or reciprocate.*

Recipients may react negatively especially when the gift or assistance is large, triggering uncomfortable feelings of indebtedness. Generous gifts can even make people feel uneasy or obligated to have a type of relationship with the giver that they wouldn't have chosen, or didn't get to choose. Large gifts and help involving great sacrifice or effort can make people feel beholden to the giver with no end in sight. Some recipients experience this as an uncomfortable relationship power imbalance and resent the giver and the gift.

Condition 3: *The way the help is delivered is perceived by the recipient as an infringement of their personal freedom.*

When people experience a loss of personal control they often become angry, reactive, and rebellious. For example, they may believe you're controlling because you put conditions on your help or dictated the terms of repayment. Some recipients experience this as a loss of personal freedom. They already feel a loss of control due to needing help. They don't appreciate giving up even more control as a condition of receiving your gift. Also, if they think you're giving so that you can tell them what they can and can't do, they may experience your gift as insincere and manipulative, and feel no obligation to behave as you demand or expect.

Some givers have good intentions, but their bossy intervention style comes off as controlling. Most people don't like to be bossed, although they'll tolerate it if they think the giver's position warrants it (for example, a manager generally has the right to tell subordinates what to do or a younger child might accept a parent's bossiness). But if the bossing is seen as illegitimate, recipients usually feel disrespected and unfairly controlled.

Regardless of our intentions, our unsolicited intervention can feel disrespectful, controlling, sanctimonious, condescending, or bossy to recipients. We may think we're only trying to help with our unsolicited advice, suggestions, or task help, but our assistance may be unwelcome and misinterpreted. Instead of our intervention being attributed to our giving nature, it may be attributed to our controlling nature and to our distrust of others to do things to our satisfaction.

It's worth noting that some people (particularly, toddlers, teens, and people with particular personality traits) are prone to perceiving helpfully intended intervention as disrespectful, bossy, or as an affront to their privacy, dignity, and personal freedom. Difficult takers may be especially contemptuous of the giver, perhaps because many have a proclivity towards *psychological reactance* (a negative reaction arising from a perceived threat to one's freedom, followed by resistance to the recommended action). Indeed, these traits often create resistance to responsible adult behavior. This, in combination with a propensity to feel easily criticized or disrespected, made worse by addiction and some types of personalities, creates a situation where they're predisposed to need and want help and to rebel against what they see as the giver's efforts to control them as a condition of receiving help.

Recipients coping with a recent loss of independence due to aging, illness, or accident may also respond negatively because the giver's intervention is a painful reminder of the loss of their independence.

Condition 4: *The recipient believes the helping or giving arises from duty and obligation, or is about impressing others, rather than arising from care and concern about them.*

For example, negative reactions are likely if the recipient believes the giver's primary motivation for helping is to make other people think they're good and nice. If the giver's sincerity is questionable in the mind of the recipient, they may act disrespectfully or ungratefully.

It's important to recognize that we have limited control over how recipients perceive our intentions or respond to our assistance and gifts. The four conditions outlined above *don't even have to be true* for recipients to react negatively. All that's required is a belief in their truth (this is one reason why negative reactions from recipients can catch givers off-guard). But negative reactions usually mean we should reconsider our giving in that relationship. This may mean:

- Pulling back on our generous gifts or help.
- Keeping our unsolicited intervention, including advice and suggestions, to ourselves.
- Showing more sensitivity when intervening, especially when recipients have experienced a loss of autonomy due to recent illness, disability, or economic misfortune like a job loss.
- Taking the "bossy" down a notch or two (or three).
- Checking our motives and our sincerity.

Box 3.3 helps you reflect on the impact of your helping and giving on your relationship with recipients.

Box 3.3 Has Your Giving/Helping Negatively Impacted Your Relationships with the Recipients?

Think about the unhealthy giving situation(s) you're in and use the scale to rate the items. Consult a friend, loved one, or therapist to assist you if needed.

1=Strongly Disagree
2=Disagree
3=Neutral
4=Agree
5=Strongly Agree

My giving/helping has negatively affected my relationship(s) with the recipient(s) of my help in the following ways:

____1. The relationship has declined.
____2. The relationship is tense.
____3. We have fewer positive interactions than we used to.
____4. We are often unpleasant towards one another.
____5. We avoid one another.
____6. I'm dissatisfied with the relationship because they haven't responded to my helping or giving as I expected.
____7. We have regular disagreements related to the helping/giving arrangements.
____8. There is uncomfortable imbalance in our relationship.
____9. Disrespect has creeped into our relationship.
____10. Resentment has creeped into our relationship.

Compute an average by adding up all your responses and dividing by 10 (an average over 4 is of greater concern than one under 3). Reflect on your responses, paying special attention to items you marked with a 4 or a 5. What does this tell you about the effects of your helping and giving on your relationship?

Harms To Givers' Other Relationships

Our unhealthy helping and giving relationships usually affect some of our other relationships, especially when others firmly believe the taker's self-reliance, maturity, or sobriety is hindered by our continued giving. When friends or loved ones are committed to not enabling the taker, they may be angry or frustrated with us for thwarting their efforts with our continued enabling. Their efforts to set boundaries when we won't also places them in the role of the bad guy, a position that would be easier to handle if we formed a unified front with them. These disagreements about how to best respond to a taker's predicament can strain relationships.

This dynamic is particularly common in families with a member addicted to drugs or alcohol. At the height of their addiction, many addicts beg and borrow (and sometimes steal) from family members to meet basic needs for food and shelter, or to get money for alcohol, drugs, or cigarettes. After being burnt a few times and learning about addiction, some givers realize their help enables the addicted family member and decreases the chances of recovery. They then become frustrated with family members that continue to rescue and provide material support to the addicted family member.

Relationships may also be hurt when our unhealthy giving leads other people in our lives to feel hurt or resentful that they're deprived of our resources or attention. For example, imagine the giver that's so devoted to a humanitarian political or social cause that they neglect important personal relationships. Or, take the parent that enables one of their children or a spouse or lover. If the enabled person gets most of the giver's attention and a disproportionate amount of family resources, the forgotten loved ones feel hurt they were deprived of care. They see this deprivation as the giver's choice and that often has long-term relationship impacts. Some years later, neglected or deprived loved ones may remain angry, distant, or disrespectful of givers that they believe made choices to help or give to others at their expense.

Finally, some friends or loved ones may withdraw from the giver if they find the giver's suffering difficult to bear. People become weary of givers that complain repeatedly but are unwilling to do anything to change the situation. They may become angry and frustrated with givers that choose to continue the unhealthy giving that appears to be destroying them. They may miss the "old" person that wasn't defined and dominated by the unhealthy giving relationship.

Relationships with friends or loved ones may become strained as they pressure the giver to set boundaries around their giving. Givers may become defensive when others disagree with their handling of the situation. They may distance from their critics, or withhold information because it's hard to admit another agreement was broken, another bailout occurred, or they're providing help they can ill-afford. Keeping such secrets adds to the giver's stress as they lose out on needed emotional support. When they lose touch with family and friends, and their relationship with the taker is one of the only relationships they have left, they become even more committed to making it work.

Box 3.4 helps you reflect on the impact of your helping and giving on your other relationships.

Box 3.4 Has Your Helping and Giving Negatively Impacted Your Other Relationships?

Think about the unhealthy helping and giving situation(s) you're in and use the scale to rate the items. Consult a friend, loved one, or therapist to assist if needed.

1=Strongly Disagree
2=Disagree
3=Neutral
4=Agree
5=Strongly Agree

My Giving/Help Has Negatively Affected My Other Relationships in the Following Ways:

____1. Friends or relatives have told me they feel I don't care about them as much as the person/people/group I help

____2. I have disagreements with friends and loved ones about my helping or giving

____3. I neglect my other relationships because of my unhealthy giving/helping relationship(s)

____4. I avoid some of my friends or loved ones because they clearly disapprove of my giving/helping relationship(s)

____5. Some of my friends or loved ones may have backed off from our relationship because they think I should stop giving or helping so much

Additional negative consequences to your relationships not listed above:

Compute an average by adding up all your responses and dividing by 5 (an average over 4 is of greater concern than one under 3). Reflect on your responses, paying special attention to items you marked with a 4 or a 5. What does this tell you about the effects of your unhealthy helping and giving on your relationships?

Harms To Groups, Work Teams, and Organizations

Being a helpful, cooperative group member is an ingredient of group, team, and organizational success. Successful organizations need good organizational citizens who help their coworkers and who voluntarily take on extra tasks and work. They need helpful people that engage in what organizational psychologists call *organizational citizenship behaviors* (OCBs). OCBs include things like picking up other employees' slack, doing favors for coworkers, switching schedules, coming in early when needed, sending cards to coworkers, helping coworkers with personal problems, and bringing food to share. Groups, teams, and organizations need people that give extra time and energy to help the group perform at a higher level. Good group and organizational citizens also inspire other members to give of themselves. This increases the group's performance and cohesion.

Helpful, giving, cooperative people are often the difference between under-performing groups and teams, and high-performing ones. However, helping and giving in a group context can be excessive and ultimately unproductive leading to giver burnout, promoting others' incompetence or laziness, and reducing productivity.

For twenty years I taught a group dynamics class where students learned about groups and teams. I assigned them to six-person teams given the goal of raising money for a community non-profit organization. Many of these teams were extremely successful and on average, each team raised $1200-$1500 in a mere six weeks, with the occasional group raising more than $2000. I monitored the groups closely, observing their functioning. I observed what went right in their groups and what went wrong, and advised and coached the fund-raising teams.

Over time I noticed that one type of under-performing group with high levels of dissatisfaction was the group with a member (or two) who took on the burden of the group's work at the outset, a form of over-helping and hyper-responsibility for the group's work that essentially cut other people out. This created a situation of workhorses and slackers which reduced group performance, and degraded the group experience. The situation almost always created bad blood between the workhorses and the slackers. Eventually it became something that I cautioned my students about letting happen on their teams. I also guarded against it as a leader and member of many committee and project groups.

Over-giving group members of this sort are often highly conscientious and take charge of the group's work to increase their sense of control and reduce their anxiety. Many seek group status and others' approval through their helpfulness. But their excessively helpful efforts often contribute to a situation where a workload that should be divided somewhat equally becomes one where a single member (the giver) is stuck with a disproportionate amount of responsibility and labor.

Givers often misattribute a skewed workload in their groups to the laziness or selfishness of their groupmates/teammates. Sometimes they're right. But other times it's actually a consequence of their taking over and doing too much. In the process of trying to be helpful to the group and its members, and/or relieve their anxiety about the job getting done to their standards, the giver inadvertently enables a group norm where people don't do their share. Members assume the giver's hyper-responsibility for group tasks means their efforts are unneeded or unwanted. So they back off and let the giver do it rather than fight about it. If you regularly find yourself living and working amongst slackers, your over-helping could be a culprit. [20]

In the workplace, an over-helping group member may unintentionally limit the job skill acquisition and job knowledge of their coworkers. Consequently, over-helping can impede others' career development. The group may also become overly dependent on the giver's labor. This can negatively affect productivity when the giver is absent due to vacation, illness, etc. In a workplace, it may take longer to get the group's work done not because they are down a person, but because a giver's over-helping enabled coworkers' limited skill sets and promoted irresponsibility. In a household, the absence of an overly-responsible member may lead to chaos when others don't know how to shop, cook, clean, do laundry, and find the toilet paper stash.

Unfortunately, promoting a group or relationship norm where one person is the workhorse and others are free riders may eventually ripen into the giver's resentment and burnout. This can sour once-friendly relations between the giver and other group members, erode the group's cohesion (members' attachment to the group and to one another), and even lead some members to leave.

Givers usually expect their large contributions to the group will lead others to like and accept them but that doesn't always happen. Although the giver means well, other group members often misperceive the giver's intent and feel disrespected. They may perceive the helper as inappropriately dominant or controlling and dislike or resent them. They also may feel angry if they believe the giver's hyper-responsibility marginalizes them, preventing their full inclusion in the group. They feel unhappy when another's over-helping means they can't share credit for team success. Meanwhile, the giver feels underappreciated and confused by the lack of gratitude. These negative feelings also reduce group cohesion.

Over-helping can also reduce the quality of the group's work, for example, when the giver can't fully compensate for the reduced contributions of other group members. An exhausted over-giver may not be able to keep up with all the housework generated by other members. Or, a group comes to depend on the giver's greater efforts but the giver becomes tired or resentful and begins to withhold it. I have heard many tales of college roommate groups, work teams, and non-profit volunteer groups where over-helping members start feeling overwhelmed and unappreciated and then retreat. The result: things don't get done or don't get done well. Unless the group adopts a new and more equitable division of labor, the story ends with people leaving due to frustration, and because the group experience is so unrewarding. [21]

One benefit of groups is that individual group members bring different skills, information, and experience to the group and this diversity can enhance group performance and the group's experience. But group performance can suffer when unique skills or information relevant to the group's goal remain untapped. Yet this is what happens if the giver does most of the group's work and leaves little room for other members' contributions. Although they may intend to serve the group by taking on a lot of the group's responsibilities, a dominant over-helper may reduce the opportunities for other people to contribute in ways that would enhance the group's product. Because working cooperatively and successfully for a group goal increases people's attachments to other group members and to the group, over-giving can also inhibit group cohesion. This is yet another case where our helpfulness ultimately proves unhelpful.

Organizational psychologist Adam Grant studied givers in the workplace and found successful workplace givers had clear parameters around who to help, how to help, and how much. [22] They assisted coworkers that used the help for greater productivity and people that "paid it forward" by helping others increase their productivity. They were less likely to help selfish taker coworkers. Although they didn't help so others would feel obligated to reciprocate, people were glad to help them when they needed it, which increased their own career success.

We can be helpful, supportive coworkers and group members without hurting the group's cohesiveness and productivity, reducing the responsibility of others, or sacrificing our own health. We should be willing to go above and beyond to signal our commitment to the group and its members, and to promote group productivity. But your giving and helpfulness may be taken advantage of in groups with "taker norms" (norms of competitiveness between group members where everyone is out for him or herself). If your high level of giving fails to inspire a giving group culture with a shared commitment to give to the group and its members, and if it leads to your overwork and resentment, it's probably best to pull back on your service to the group.

Grant notes that it's also best to assist the group members that share your cooperative, helpful philosophy and not to help the takers that are largely about their own personal gain. Although takers aren't always immediately obvious because some act as fake givers—doing things for others but only so that they can ask for something in return later—they can't hide their "takeriness" forever. Be on the lookout for people that only help when there's something in it for them (they are just takers dressed in givers' clothing). And finally, make sure your help doesn't prevent others from being full, contributing members of the group or society. If your help doesn't inspire and promote others' productivity and just makes it easy for them to slack, you're providing the wrong kind of help, or you're trying to help a taker.

Box 3.5 helps you consider the group impacts of your helping and giving.

Box 3.5 Has Your Helping/Giving Impacted Your Groups?

1. Do you have a tendency to do more than your share of work in situations where a group of people needs to accomplish something? Can you give some examples?
2. If you tend to do more than your fair share in group situations, describe any resulting negative consequences. For example, explain how this affected your health, relationships with other group members, whether it's made the group dependent on your labor and any problems resulting from that, and how it's affected the quantity and quality of the group's work.

These first three chapters clarified what unhealthy (dysfunctional) helping and giving are, what types of things unhealthy helpers and givers do, and the negative consequences of unhealthy helping and giving. The next five chapters examine psychological explanations for unhealthy helping and giving, explaining *why* people do it. These explanations are interesting and promote insight, but their biggest advantage is that they translate into practical strategies for personal change.

Four

The Personality Traits of Unhealthy Givers

Why are some people more prone to unhealthy helping and giving than others? Psychological research suggests it's partly because some people possess a potent combination of personality traits that predispose them to respond to others' distress with unhealthy helping and giving. Personality traits affect what people feel, think, and do in response to potential helping and giving situations and affect *prosociality* (a person's enduring tendencies to share, help, and provide care to others).

Positive psychologists Christopher Peterson and Martin Seligman say selfless helping is part of the human character strength (virtue) called "humanity." They say research shows selfless helpers are typically empathic sympathizers who engage in other-centered moral reasoning and believe they have a personal ethical responsibility to help. [23] Many over-helpers and over-givers probably have an intensified *prosocial personality orientation,* described by social psychologists Louis Penner and Marcia Finkelstein as an enduring tendency to think about the welfare and rights of other people, to feel concern and empathy, and to act in ways that benefit others. [24] [25] When combined with certain other personality traits, family dynamics, and emotional issues like those described in the next chapter, these traits can set people up for helping and giving trouble.

The Personality Traits of Rescuers

Heroic rescue is typically a selfless act arising out of strength, virtue, and good character. Rescuing is valuable. It saves lives and prevents and reduces suffering. The willingness of some people to put themselves at risk to save others stands in stark contrast to humans' many selfish and aggressive tendencies. We revere heroic rescuers and they deserve it. They are proof of human goodness in the face in human badness, providing a silver lining to some of life's harshest human storm clouds.

I suspect many unhealthy rescuers share the personality traits of the people in Nazi-occupied territories that took great risks to save their Jewish neighbors. Consider this study by researcher Elizabeth Midlarsky and her colleagues. [26] Several decades after World War II they compared the personality traits of non-Jewish heroes of the Holocaust with non-rescuers (bystanders who didn't intervene and prewar immigrants to the United States).

The researchers found the rescuers were independent people with an internal locus of control (a belief that they had personal control over life events). They were highly empathic, easily taking another's perspective and understanding how someone else might feel. They were the type of risk-takers willing to take on risks or challenges for things they felt were important. When considering dilemmas involving others they thought about the greater good. They believed helping less fortunate others was the right thing to do. Their action was fueled by these traits (empathy, internal locus of control, risk-taking, social responsibility, and other-oriented morality).

Many unhealthy rescuers have these traits. The difference is they're heroic rescuers gone wrong. Although well-intended, they regularly make poor rescuing choices and launch unwarranted and ill-fated rescues. They misdiagnose other people's situations as emergencies requiring their intervention. They rescue and try to fix difficult takers. They assume too much responsibility for solving other people's problems, thinking their intervention can fix people's complicated problems that were years in the making. They rescue in ways that enable rather than empower. They impulsively intervene before others have a chance to empower themselves by finding their own solutions, and when in the long run, others won't benefit from their intervention.

Unhealthy Helping and The Five Factor Theory of Personality

Psychologists recently synthesized the many personality traits identified by research into five basic dimensions. Known as the five-factor model (FFM) of personality, it's one of the hottest things in the study of personality and for good reason. Not only is it research-based, but it does a good job describing how people's personalities may differ. [27] The FFM personality categories or factors (which conveniently spell out "OCEAN") are *Openness* (O), *Conscientiousness* (C), *Extraversion* (E), *Agreeableness* (A), and *Neuroticism* (N). Two of these, agreeableness and neuroticism, are particularly relevant to unhealthy helping and giving.

Agreeableness

Agreeableness (A) is probably the factor most related to unhealthy helping and giving. High-A individuals are forgiving, generous, kind, caring, sympathetic, trusting, and altruistic while low-A individuals are more spiteful, self-centered, and indifferent to other people's difficulties. Two prominent FFM personality researchers, Paul Costa and Robert McCrae, define the altruistic (selfless helping) feature of agreeableness as an active concern for others' welfare as shown in generosity, consideration of others, and a willingness to assist others in need of help.

In a series of studies, social psychologist William Graziano and his team found motivations to behave prosocially were positively correlated with agreeableness. When they systematically varied helping situations and compared people high on the agreeableness personality factor with people low on the agreeableness factor, they found people high in agreeableness were more helpful to friends and siblings in everyday situations (e.g., helping with a car breakdown) and more likely to help strangers in extraordinary helping situations (e.g., entering a burning house to save someone). People low in agreeableness weren't emotionally unresponsive to victims. They just experienced the victims' suffering in a more self-centered way than those high in agreeableness, helping only when costs were low. In general, people high in agreeableness were less discriminating in regards to whom to help and when, and more likely to help even when helping costs were high. [28]

Forgivingness

Research also finds that high agreeableness is associated with forgivingness, a personality tendency to be forgiving of others' transgressions against us, especially when the relationship is a close one. [29] This tendency to forgive those that have taken advantage of us, not kept agreements, or even manipulated us, may promote long-term codependent and unhealthy helping and giving relationships.

Compared to being unforgiving, which typically involves anger, bitterness, and resentment and has negative mental health and physical health effects, being "forgiving" is associated with positive health outcomes. But like many otherwise positive traits, forgivingness has a downside. In the case of high-A unhealthy helpers, forgivingness sometimes translates into forgiving others' many broken promises and prolonged underperformance, and accepting questionable excuses. Forgivingness can delay needed boundary setting.

Empathy and Selfless Helping

The agreeableness personality factor includes the trait of empathy and if research tells us anything about the helpful personality it's that helpful people are empathic. They're more likely to react to other people's problems or distress due to a heightened ability to take the perspective of others. Strongly empathic people more easily feel what others are feeling and are more emotionally affected by others' suffering. This sympathy and compassion makes them more likely to take responsibility for the welfare of others and act to help them. [30] Usually, they have personal values consistent with helping less fortunate others.[31] Empathy is also associated with high levels of arousal that interfere with our ability to consider the potential costs of helping. This means that we're more likely to impulsively and heroically intervene when empathy is strong. [32]

Social psychologist C. Daniel Batson suggests true selfless helping (altruism) only occurs when there's empathy for another; otherwise, we'll only help if the rewards of helping outweigh the costs. [33] For example, even without empathy, we may help because people will think poorly of us if we don't, or positively of us if we do, because we'll feel guilty if we don't, or because it's our duty. In the absence of empathy, we may not help if it's inconvenient or monetarily expensive, unless the rewards of helping outweigh these costs.

I think you'll agree that people with a consistent pattern of unhealthy helping and giving are often strong empathic responders. They experience intense feelings and emotional arousal when they perceive someone is in need. Feeling another's pain and wanting to alleviate it, they impulsively rescue, help, and give. Empathy also makes it more difficult for them to set and follow through with helping limits because they vicariously experience the stress their boundaries create for the other person.

My empathy certainly contributed to the pinnacle of my long unhealthy helping and giving career. In 2009, my sister Charlie and her husband faced financial ruin as the economy tanked and their small business suffered. Meanwhile, my sister's health deteriorated and she couldn't work. Then they lost their house to foreclosure. They needed to move but couldn't find an affordable rental home that allowed pets. It pained me to watch them struggle and I worried horribly about their fate. I found their distress absolutely heart breaking and I became practically obsessed with helping them.

So, wanting to make things better, my husband and I offered to buy a house for them to rent and live in. Although our resources were limited, I felt compelled to act to alleviate their suffering. Problems arose almost instantly due to the dual relationship, but we remained committed. Within a year, rent subsidies, home repair, and maintenance costs strained our finances but my husband and I hung in there. Then health issues led to my husband's early retirement, leading us to the difficult decision to sell the house after three years. By this time my sister's financial fortunes had improved and they could find an acceptable place to rent without our assistance, so this isn't as heartless as it sounds, but it was difficult for us all. I still don't know if offering this type of help was the best thing to do. They probably would've been fine without our assistance, and our relationship may have been better off had we not intervened. What I do know is that my empathy made me hell-bent on doing it.

I love my sister which partly explains my willingness to help in the way I did. Indeed, some psychological research suggests that our emotional empathy is most intense when there's kinship (family ties), a close relationship, or a strong identification with the other due to shared group membership (the person is a member of our tribe). This is yet another thing that makes family relationships enabling-prone. [34]

Before offering help, we make an assessment about the deservingness of the "victim" and whether they're responsible for needing help—we ask ourselves if the cause of the problem is under the person's control. If we believe the cause of the other's need is uncontrollable, such that they couldn't prevent it, we feel sympathy and we are more likely to help. If we believe that they bear personal responsibility, then we feel anger or irritation, and are less likely to help. [35]

But when it's a close relationship, we're more likely to believe another's poor situation is due to forces beyond their control rather than their own poor choices, for we don't want to think badly of someone dear to us. We tend to cut people we like and care about a lot of slack when making attributions about their need for help. Even in the face of contrary evidence we're likely to make situational attributions for the close other's misfortune ("It's not their fault!"). Or, when we do acknowledge their role in creating their problems, our love and care for them leads us to empathize with them anyway, and want to relieve their suffering ("Poor baby is having a hard time!").

If we're close to the other, we're also more likely to know about possible extenuating circumstances, disabilities, or addictions. For example, when the relationship is close and we know of past uncontrollable traumatic events in the life of the other, we may attribute their failure to function normally to these events. This makes them seem more deserving of our help. [36]

Box 4.1 helps you consider your empathic responding tendencies.

Box 4.1 Are You an Empath?

Use the scale to rate the items.

1=Strongly Disagree
2=Disagree
3=Neutral
4=Agree
5=Strongly Agree

_____1. Other people's suffering easily disturbs me.
_____2. I'm quick to tear up when watching emotional scenes on TV or in the movies.
_____3. I'm inclined to feel distressed when someone tells me of their troubles.
_____4. The problems of other people often concern me greatly.
_____5. People that know me would probably say that I'm a compassionate person.
_____6. I can easily relate to the difficulties of other people.
_____7. I feel the joys and pains expressed by the people around me.
_____8. I'm usually one of the first people to notice that someone else is having a difficult time.
_____9. When I see a troubled person, I feel worry or sadness.
_____10. I find it easy to put myself in someone else's shoes and imagine what they're going through.

Scoring: Add up all your scores and divide by 10. The closer your score is to 5, the more empathic your tendencies.

Empathy and Selfish Helping

I'm tempted to claim my empathy leads to helpfulness that's Jesus-like in its selflessness. But the truth is that sometimes my giving is probably about relieving my own suffering as much as it's about relieving someone else's. My empathic nature can lead me to experience others' difficulties almost as if they were my own. I then become very concerned and provide assistance to relieve my own anxiety.

Indeed, Batson, and other social psychologists, such as Robert Cialdini, admit that emotional empathy can motivate egoistic (selfish) helping when the helping is motivated by a desire to relieve our own internal distress arising from our empathy. This is called the *negative affect theory of helping*. Applied to our topic of unhealthy helping, the idea is that our empathy creates distress and anxiety. It's painful to see the other person struggle or in crisis and this makes us impulsively act to relieve that distress. This perspective suggests that in some cases, our helping may be an effort to reduce our own distress as much as it's about truly helping others.

Making Empathy and Agreeableness A Strength Rather Than A Curse

Psychologists Thomas Widiger and Jennifer Presnall note that while the agreeableness trait of altruism is generally a good thing, it can be extremely maladaptive.

For example, the helpfulness and generosity of high-A people can have tremendous negative consequences, including victimization and abuse. [37] A helper's high-A traits may even lead to codependent relationships with low-A takers that meet criteria for personality disorders like anti-social personality disorder, borderline personality disorder, and personality disorders involving narcissist traits. Recently, researchers have linked low agreeableness to these personality disorders. [38]

Once again, helping is a great and wonderful thing but it can be excessive, unnecessary, unhealthy, and counterproductive. If you're a high-A person, beware so this personality trait doesn't lead you into unhealthy helping and giving.

Box 4.2 Could Being High-A Compromise Your Comfortable Retirement?

A recent study from the American investment firm Merrill Lynch should cause high-A people to pause, especially as they near or enter retirement. The study found six in ten people aged fifty and older provide monetary support to family members such as parents, adult children, or siblings (on average $14,900 a year). A majority (80%) said they helped their relatives because "it was the right thing to do." Three out of five people can identify a family member as the "family bank," to whom other members turn for help. This role was typically assigned to the family member that saved and invested and had the most money, and was most approachable. If you ask me, these family banks sound like high-A individuals.

Sixty percent of people approaching retirement age said they would push back their own retirement to help family members. Forty percent said they would return to work after retirement or accept a less comfortable retirement to assist family.

Another interesting study finding was that some people closed the doors of their family bank. Most (57%) did this because they felt the money wasn't being used wisely, but others (about one-third), because their own lifestyle was suffering.

Source: *The Family and Retirement: The Elephant in the Room A Merrill Lynch Retirement Study conducted in partnership with Age Wave* (http://wealthmanagement.ml.com/publish/content/application/pdf/GWMOL/Merrill-Lynch-2013-Family-and-Retirement-Study.pdf) (http://wealthmanagement.ml.com/publish/content/application/pdf/GWMOL/Merrill-Lynch-2013-Family-and-Retirement-Study.pdf)

Although personality traits are by definition relatively stable and enduring, that doesn't mean that we can't do anything to tone down their potential negative effects. In this case, it's worth acknowledging that one of our best qualities is also one of our worst. For example, your empathy and other-centeredness are largely a good thing since the people you care about, the people you work with, and even complete strangers, may legitimately need your help sometimes. Your selflessness and willingness to help qualify you as a genuinely nice person of good character. But untamed, these qualities bring trouble. You can be too quick to empathize, you can empathize too much, and your empathy can lead to impulsive rescuing when rescuing isn't the best thing to do. And, your agreeableness can lead to excessive self-sacrifice.

But you can keep your empathy from leading you astray. I've learned that when my impulse is strong, I can't act automatically from my emotions.

Instead, when I sense another's distress I prepare to override my empathic impulse long enough to make a reasoned decision about whether it's really best. In Chapter 6, I'll talk about this switch from automatic to thoughtful processing as switching from Cognitive System 1 to Cognitive System 2. It's often an important part of healthy helping and giving.

Of course impulsive rescuing is sometimes the best thing to do. Quick bystander intervention saves lives and reduces harm. You should snatch a baby out of the street before an oncoming car hits it. I also support: intervening to stop a sexual predator about to take advantage of an intoxicated or underage person, performing cardiopulmonary resuscitation on a person having a heart attack, doing something to stop a bully, tackling a gunman about to open fire in a public place, and stopping terrorists from igniting bombs in their underwear.

But if it's not really a life or death situation, make an effort to calm your emotional arousal (try some deep breaths, a walk, some tea) and assess the situation. Switch to your conscious, thinking side. Think about whether you can physically, emotionally, or financially afford to offer this help. Consider whether your help or rescue is really even needed or wanted, and whether it's likely to be effective. Question whether your help will enable another's immaturity, addiction, or irresponsibility. Help or give only if it's really the best thing to do.

Remember too, that when people tell you of their troubles, they're not always looking for rescue. Sometimes they just need to vent, talk over their options, or get reassurance it'll be okay and they can handle it. As my husband points out, most of the time people do just fine without our help so there's nothing wrong with saying "uh-huh" and nodding sympathetically when someone tells you their tale of woe. Caring doesn't necessarily require you intervene to solve another's problems. Just because you feel empathy doesn't necessarily mean you *should* take responsibility or that you *need* to take responsibility for fixing the situation (in Chapter 7, this is called an *emotional reasoning mindtrap*).

Finally, when you set a needed boundary expect your empathy might tempt you to soften, especially if your boundary creates difficulties for the other. Reminding yourself that this discomfort is a normal, but temporary, part of the boundary-setting process may help. To manage the boundary guilt resulting from your empathy, remind yourself why your boundaries are necessary (refer back to Chapter 3 for some sobering reminders) or, ask a trusted friend familiar with the situation to remind you. Chapters 8, 9, and 10 also provide tips for managing boundary guilt and ambivalence.

You can think more about how your empathy influences your helping and giving by answering the questions in Box 4.3.

Box 4.3 Are You A Fool That Rushes in Where Angels Fear to Tread?

1. Could your helping be as much about relieving your distress as it is about relieving others' distress?
2. Is it possible that you're too quick to offer help and rescue others?
3. Can you think of incidents where you wish you'd waited before impulsively making some generous offer of help?
4. Can you think of times where your empathy led you to intervene but in retrospect, your help probably wasn't needed or appreciated?
5. What role does your empathy play in making it difficult for you to set and maintain boundaries?
6. How can you better manage your empathy so it doesn't trap you into unhealthy helping and giving?

Neuroticism

Individuals high on the personality factor of *neuroticism (N)* are anxious, tense, self-conscious worriers who may experience anxiety, depression, and low self-esteem. In contrast to high-N people, low-N people are calmer, more relaxed, and more emotionally stable. I think it's probable that people high in empathy (high-A) and prone to anxiety (high-N) are more likely to worry excessively about the lives of others. The neuroticism may also amplify the empathy because anxiety increases physiological arousal. This combination may fuel impulsive rescuing.

Self-Esteem

Self-esteem is the part of the self that consists of a person's positive and negative self-evaluations—in other words, it's the ways you judge yourself positively or negatively. Five factor personality theorists say trait self-esteem falls under the neuroticism personality factor and people high in neuroticism often have low self-esteem. Social psychologists say we need self-esteem. According to social psychology's *terror management theory*, people need to believe they're valuable and living meaningful lives so that there is a point to their existence and a purpose for their being.

We say someone has low self-esteem when they think of themselves in mostly negative terms (such as "bad" or "incompetent") and we say a person has high self-esteem when they view themselves in largely positive terms (such as "good" and "competent"). Many people with low self-esteem have incorporated other people's negative views of them into their self-view. They think they're worthless because parents or other important people told them so. Or they assume they're bad because they were abused or neglected in some way, usually by their parents ("I must be no good or why would I be treated this way?"). Some people have low self-esteem due to unrealistic, perfectionist ideals of who they should be. Because perfection is impossible, they struggle to feel good about themselves. Parents that withhold approval are often the source of a person's perception that perfection is necessary for their worthiness.

Most research on self-esteem and prosociality finds that higher levels of prosociality are correlated with higher levels of self-esteem. According to research, people inclined to share, help, and provide care to others tend to have higher, rather than lower self-esteem. For communally-oriented people (people inclined to give care to others), caring for others is a source of self-esteem. [39] Helping can also promote feelings of competence that can boost self-esteem. [40]

But the relationship between self-esteem and helping may be different when it comes to unhealthy forms of helping. Some unhealthy helping and giving is probably fueled by a desire to validate self-worth and gain acceptance and admiration from others. Low self-esteem is associated with feelings that one isn't valued by or valuable to other people. Unhealthy givers with low self-esteem may engage in excessive self-sacrifice on behalf of others in a quest to feel worthy and valuable and to feel their lives have purpose and meaning. They may base feeling good about themselves on the extent to which others like and approve of them. They intend their extreme helping and giving to win other people's love and approval.

Because people with low self-esteem lack confidence, they're often easier to persuade and quick to waver when challenged. Perhaps this makes people with low self-esteem more susceptible to unhealthy helping relationships with people who manipulate to get others to take care of them. Also, because they put a low value on themselves, unhealthy givers with low self-esteem may not believe their own suffering, discomfort, or inconvenience justifies setting helping and giving boundaries. People with low self-esteem may also feel undeserving and guilty about having resources and therefore more likely to give them away. They may let recipients treat them badly because it's consistent with how they feel about themselves (they think they deserve maltreatment).

It's even possible that some unhealthy givers choose relationships with under-functioning people requiring their near-constant support and assistance so they can feel competent and together by comparison. Leon Festinger's *social comparison theory* suggests that people often compare themselves to those that are worse off (downward social comparison) to boost their own feelings of worth. [41]

In 2013 my student Pamela Sheffler and I asked 101 adults to complete a standard measure of self-esteem, a commonly used measure of the five personality factors (OCEAN), and a measure of dysfunctional helping I created (see Box 4.4). What we found was that high neuroticism, high agreeableness, and low self-esteem were all associated with higher levels of dysfunctional helping. Together, agreeableness, neuroticism, and self-esteem explained about a quarter of the variation in dysfunctional helping (roughly speaking, that means that 75% of dysfunctional helping is determined by other variables). Self-esteem was the largest contributor, explaining about 14% of the variance in dysfunctional helping above and beyond the other variables. These are statistically significant results and suggest these personality variables influence unhealthy helping. However, more research with larger and more diverse samples is needed for more definitive conclusions. [42]

Box 4.4 Dysfunctional Helping Measure

Instructions. Please use the scale to indicate how much you agree or disagree with the statements.

1=Strongly Disagree
2=Disagree
3=Neutral
4=Agree
5=Strongly Agree

____1. I often rescue people I know from their self-imposed troubles.
____2. I tend to have one-sided relationships where I am the "giver" and others are the "takers."
____3. I instantly offer help to people I know without thinking and later regret it.
____4. If someone I know has a problem, I immediately intervene to help solve it.
____5. I tend to have relationships with people that are characterized by their crisis and my rescuing.
____6. My helpfulness and giving to the people I know means I sometimes have trouble meeting my own needs.
____7. I assist friends or family members that need help because they don't properly manage a mental or physical health condition or addiction.
____8. My helpfulness and giving have strained my financial resources.

____9. My help has probably enabled another's irresponsibility by protecting them from the normal consequences of irresponsible choices and actions.

____10. My help has probably enabled another's incompetence because they haven't had to take care of themselves.

____11. My help has probably fostered others' unhealthy dependence on me.

____12. Some of my friends or loved ones may have backed off from our relationship because they think I should stop giving or helping so much.

____13. I sometimes find myself helping even when I don't have the time, energy, or money.

____14. My giving/helping has negatively affected my relationships with the recipients of my help.

____15. People who know me well think my helping and giving are unhealthy.

Many people assume that codependence is driven by low self-esteem. However, research support for this idea is mixed and some studies find no relationship between self-esteem and codependency. [43] As I mentioned before, contradictory findings are common in the codependence research partly because how it's conceptualized and measured vary from study to study. It's also unclear whether codependent people truly have low self-esteem or whether they just obtain their self-worth partly by conforming to the abusive and exploitive demands of difficult people such as those with addictions or personality disorders.

If you ask me, unhealthy helping and giving is sometimes motivated by the pursuit of self-esteem. But if people seek self-esteem through their dysfunctional helping and giving, problems are likely. One problem with boosting your self-esteem by making excessive sacrifices for others so that you can feel saintly and giving, or so other people will think you are, is that it's usually unsustainable. It requires an ongoing pattern of self-sacrifice and a string of unhealthy helping and giving relationships. I don't know about you, but I wouldn't call that a healthy source of self-esteem! Likewise, obtaining self-esteem by feeling superior to the incompetent others you help isn't exactly the healthiest way to feel good about yourself.

Social psychologists Jennifer Crocker and Lora Parker highlight another problem. They say when compassion, kindness, altruism, and generosity are motivated by self-esteem concerns, their benefits to others are often diminished because the person is more preoccupied with what the behavior means about themselves *than they are focused on what others really need.* They give the simple example of a woman who feels good about herself because she bakes cookies for senior citizens. But she sometimes delivers cookies to people who neither need nor want them, and recipients of these kind acts sometimes feel put on the spot—they would like to refuse the cookies but find it awkward to say so. [44] Perhaps this explains why some people are hell-bent on helping or giving when others don't need or want their help or gifts, and when they help or give in unwelcome ways.

Personality Doesn't Doom Us to Unhealthy Giving

Don't feel discouraged if you believe you have some personality traits associated with unhealthy helping and giving. Fortunately, these same traits, when tamed, lead to healthy helping and giving. We can use self-knowledge and self-monitoring to keep the potentially unhealthy aspects of our personalities under control. We can check our empathy so it doesn't lead to impulsive, unsustainable helping and giving. We can tone down our forgivingness so that we don't cut too much slack to undeserving people. We can work on developing more stable and sustainable sources of self-esteem. [45] And when our short-term handup starts looking like a long term handout, and our gut (and maybe our friends, relatives, or therapist) tell us our giving is unhealthy, we can take action to set healthy boundaries.

Finally, it's important to remember that personality is only one influence on unhealthy helping and giving. In fact, most people, regardless of their personality, find themselves in an unhealthy helping and giving situation at some point.

Five

Unconscious and Emotional Influences on Unhealthy Helping and Giving

The divorce was a surprise to homemaker Jenny. Initiated by her husband who fell in love with another woman, it hit her like a sucker punch to the belly. It's a bit of an understatement to say she didn't take it well. Angry and depressed, she was all girl-gone-wild, partying night after night. Needless to say, this wasn't a good fit with her parenting responsibilities. Then she got involved with Carlton, an abusive man that moved into her home and terrorized the household with his violent moods. Caught up in her single life and budding drug addiction, she overlooked her children's school truancy (and enabled it by making excuses for them), and minimized the early drug and alcohol use of her young teen son and daughter. None of her three children graduated from high school and all were massive underachievers. Now adults, one lived with her and didn't pay rent or utilities and the other two boomeranged in and out of her house and when there, didn't contribute to the household. All three owed her lots of money.

Her father left the family when she was five, and her husband left after nineteen years of marriage, so Jenny doubted anyone could truly love her. This fear drove her to keep her adult children dependent so they wouldn't abandon her. Her unhealthy helping and giving were also driven by a lingering sense of guilt. Although Jenny mended her partying and irresponsible ways, she felt terrible about what she put her children through and how they turned out. She felt their addictions and irresponsibility were her fault and bailing them out, her responsibility.

This chapter focuses on people like Jenny who foster and maintain dependencies in others to satisfy unhealthy needs arising from unresolved emotional issues. The psychological approach that emphasizes these unconscious influences on behavior is called the *psychoanalytic or psychodynamic perspective* and it's most often associated with Sigmund Freud (who lived from 1856-1939). Basically, the work of psychoanalysts suggests that unhealthy helping and giving is shaped by patterns of interpersonal interactions during infancy and early childhood, a perspective now known as *object relations.* [46] For example, Jenny's fears of abandonment, originating in childhood abandonment by a parent, drove her to keep loved ones close by enabling them.

A product of his times, most people agree it's best to take Sigmund Freud with a grain of salt (or perhaps a whole salt shaker) since he said some ridiculous things, especially in regards to the psychology of women. However, he deserves credit for some ideas that greatly influenced the discipline of psychology and our understanding of human behavior. One Freudian idea relevant to our discussion is that we're driven partly by emotional issues, most originating in childhood, that remain outside of conscious awareness. Freud argued these deeply buried emotional issues seek expression and often bleed into our lives, saturating our relationships without our even knowing it. [47]

Freud's tri-partite (three-part) conception of the personality as comprised of what he called the id, ego, and superego was also one of the first personality theories in psychology. According to what's now called *ego psychology,* the *id* is the dark, selfish, unconscious, pleasure-seeking part of our personality driven to satisfy our sexual and aggressive instincts. Some takers, for example, might have out-of-control ids driving them to seek instant gratification, behave selfishly, and take advantage of us. The id seeks pleasure and doesn't want to work or wait for it.

The *superego* is that part of the personality representing the moral standards of society as conveyed by a person's parents. It's basically our conscience and compels our moral and responsible behavior. For instance, some givers might have strong superegos compelling them towards selfless sacrifice in the service of others. Their harsh inner critic tells them they're bad or selfish if they don't intervene to solve other people's problems or give away their resources. Like the id, the superego affects us without our conscious awareness of its influence.

The *ego* includes the part of the personality that's conscious and concerned with making decisions, controlling impulses, and perceiving and responding to reality. But the ego also includes an unconscious element that distorts reality to avoid painful emotional issues or information that threatens self-esteem. These distortions are called *defense mechanisms.* For example, due to its painfulness, a giver may unconsciously block (repress) the evidence that her son is taking advantage of her and her help is enabling his addictions. Because conscious awareness of these facts is too painful, she can't see what's obvious to other people.

Early on, psychoanalysts noted that some people appeared to be neurotically driven to do for others. In 1924, Freud wrote about "moral masochists" and in 1936, Anna Freud (his daughter and an important thinker in her own right), described such individuals as exhibiting "altruistic surrender." [48] [49] She suggested that due to a strong superego some people feel they must suppress their own wishes and desires. That's because an overly dominant superego can be puritanical and strict, leading to self-denial, and martyr-like and masochistic tendencies. This type of masochism involves inviting suffering into your life by helping and giving too much and then feeling morally superior due to the denial of your own needs for the sake of others. [50]

Anna Freud would probably see takers as stand-ins (proxies) for the giver's unacceptable wishes and desires. The care, concern, and rescuing they provide to others is what they secretly desire but think they don't deserve or shouldn't want. For example, some givers didn't receive much support from loved ones and now over-correct in their other relationships, trying to give others what they missed.

Self-Defeating Personality Disorder and Unhealthy Helping and Giving

When helping others assumes a pathological level, interfering with relationships and well being, some modern psychoanalysts might see it as evidence of a *masochistic (self-defeating) personality disorder*. According to the *Psychodynamic Diagnostic Manual (PDM)*, people with this disorder generally display sensitivity to rejection and loss, feel inferior, suffer from unconscious guilt, inhibit their anger towards others, and are more interested in receiving sympathy for their suffering than they are in resolving the problem. [51] They're said to act as though their sacrifice for others makes them morally superior to others. For them, suffering is associated with feeling good about themselves.

Because they need their suffering and victimization, we might expect that helpers with a self-defeating personality won't show an interest in changing themselves, or the situation. They may even get angry when it's suggested that they or the taker can change. Instead, they prefer to receive sympathy and admiration for their martyr-like suffering.

The psychodynamic perspective also suggests that unhealthy helping and giving may be motivated by an unconscious desire to feel connected to and cared for by others. In the *PDM* this type of self-defeating personality pattern is called *relational masochistic.* I should mention that some takers use their poor functioning to gain the attention, care, and support they lacked in childhood. Their irresponsibility and regular crises lead to rescues and interventions, which to them, prove people care about them. They too may unconsciously believe their suffering is necessary for closeness, and for receiving love and attention from friends and family.

How Guilt Can Drive Unhealthy Helping and Giving

According to the psychodynamic approach, our behavior is often driven by unconscious motives. Along these lines, some people feel guilty about their past actions and this guilt drives them to atone for their sins by helping and giving. These givers are driven by an unconscious need to reduce their guilt by making reparations for past mistakes affecting the taker, or to settle other karmic debts accrued from past bad behavior. Later in the chapter, you'll see this is a form of the ego defense mechanism called *compensation.*

Dissonance, in the form of regret and guilt, may arise long after our original act and motivate unhealthy helping and giving. Even when we experienced little regret or guilt at the time we may grow and mature such that past choices are highly inconsistent with the person we are now. The resulting guilt and regret (dissonance) can sometimes lead to dysfunctional helping and giving as we try to make it right. Guilt as an unhealthy giving motivator seems particularly common among parents who deeply regret neglecting or abusing their children during childhood, or who feel guilty for failing to protect their children from some sort of abuse. This guilt unconsciously motivates maladaptive giving to their children.

For example, Ken was a father who drank heavily when his children were young. He was a serial disappointing daddy, missing important family events like birthdays, and school and athletic performances. Now sober, his guilt over his past parenting led him to heavily enable his now adult children. He bought houses for them to live in and provided employment for them. Like many guilty parents, he gave freely and often in the hopes of making amends for his mistakes and gaining his children's forgiveness.

Box 5.1 helps you consider the role of guilt in your helping and giving.

Box 5.1 Guilt As An Unhealthy Helping and Giving Motivator

Honestly rate each statement with the following scale:

1=Strongly Disagree
2=Disagree
3=Neutral
4=Agree
5=Strongly Agree

As you go along, take detailed notes to elaborate on items you agreed with.

____1. I have deep regrets about how my past behavior affected those I love and giving generously helps me make it up to them.
____2. I hope that if I give enough, I'll be forgiven for my past mistakes that hurt others.
____3. I hope my generosity proves that I'm no longer the person I was.
____4. I feel like I need to make up for my past behavior through my generosity.
____5. I deserve to pay heavily to compensate for how I hurt others.

Scoring: Average your scores. The closer your average is to 5, the more this is an issue for you. What does your score, and the notes you made as you went along, tell you?

If you recognize that past guilt plays a role in your current unhealthy helping and giving, consider trying to forgive yourself. While it's important to take your share of responsibility for the harms you caused to others, you don't have to overdo it and become a doormat to pay for your mistakes.

On the one hand, if you made choices that hurt people important to you, then perhaps you should take responsibility and apologize to those people. To do that effectively, be careful not to minimize or dismiss their historical experience of you and how they say it affected them. You may want to explain any circumstances that led to your poor choices but be careful not to imply you shouldn't be held responsible (for example, blaming it on an addiction, a job, a bad childhood, an ex, or their difficult behavior). Remember you were an adult, and to the people you hurt, your actions were choices you made that you should take responsibility for. To deny or minimize that invites anger and hurt. You can make amends by being mature, loving, and supportive, without assuming full responsibility for their present life and choices.

On the other hand, it's obvious you weren't exactly a pillar of good mental health and maturity. So in some sense, the choices made of your own free will weren't so free. You made poor decisions that affected other people because you didn't have the skills (or good mental health) to respond maturely to the challenges you faced. Can you forgive your past broken self and be proud of your current self? How long and how much must you pay for your past sins? If you have indeed recognized the errors of your past ways and changed your life, perhaps it's time to ease up on the guilt, especially if it's driving you to do things that interfere with others' personal growth and maturity, or your physical, emotional, and financial health.

Forgiving yourself may also apply to regrets about your past unhealthy helping and giving. In retrospect it's obvious you made poor helping and giving choices but hindsight is, as they say, 20/20. You didn't know then what you know now and weren't then who you are now. What matters now is that you've changed and you're making better choices.

How Fears of Abandonment and Rejection Can Drive Unhealthy Helping and Giving

Many psychoanalysts emphasize that problems in the parent-child relationship set the stage for problems in our later relationships. Psychoanalyst Karen Horney (1855-1952) suggested that parental indifference leads to neurotic needs, like a neurotic need to please others and be liked by them, and a neurotic need to get others to live as you think they should. [52] These two neurotic needs in particular may motivate unhealthy helping and giving. Some of us are people-pleasers that over-help and over-give to gain people's affections. Others of us are controlling over-helpers, motivated by strong beliefs about what others and we must do.

Object-relations theory proposes that how we experience and respond in relationships is a reflection of early love attachments, especially attachments to our parents. For example, due to parental neglect or parental absence during their childhoods, some people have fears of abandonment that color their later relationships. When applied to our topic, the idea is that these fears of rejection and abandonment (originating in early relationships) may drive people to use their helping and giving to keep other people close.

It's often said that codependent people have abandonment fears. Think about it this way: people insecure about their lovability may think incentives are needed to get people to enter and stay in a relationship with them. They use their helping and giving to promote intimacy and contact with others they fear won't happen otherwise. They unconsciously want their help to bind people to them. If they're unnecessary to the other person, they fear they'll be abandoned or rejected. So they make themselves indispensable and foster dependency so the other person can't live without them.

Some givers resist withdrawing their aid because they fear finding out that the aid (rather than love and regard for them) is why the other stays. Maura was a case in point. She grew up in a family where love was withdrawn if she wasn't the perfect, devoted daughter her mother and father could display to people they wanted to impress. This made her feel she might be abandoned at any time. When Maura's son James and daughter-in-law April had a baby, Maura showered them with gifts, and helped with bills. The recently retired Maura took care of her grandchild while his parents worked. When they had another baby, they expected Maura to do the same and a little bit more. Again Maura complied without complaint even as she struggled with fatigue and drew down her retirement account to help them. When Maura heard they were pregnant again, she felt despair—how could she afford to help support another grandchild and where would she find the energy to watch and clean up after three children? Meanwhile, James and April had no idea how Maura felt and assumed that she was okay with the arrangement.

Box 5.2 helps you to think about the role of abandonment and rejection issues in your rescuing and enabling.

Box 5.2 Fears of Abandonment As An Unhealthy Helping and Giving Motivator

Honestly rate each statement with the following scale:

1=Strongly Disagree
2=Disagree
3=Neutral
4=Agree
5=Strongly Agree

As you go along, take detailed notes to elaborate on items you agreed with.

____1. I fear that people may not want to have a relationship with me if I don't give them things or do things for them.
____2. I was ignored or neglected by a parent.
____3. I was left by a parent.
____4. My parent's(s') words or deeds made me/make me feel like I was/am unlovable.
____5. I like to be needed by others because it keeps them in a relationship with me.

Scoring: Compute an average score by adding your scores and dividing by the number of items. A score between 4 and 5 suggests that this is an issue for you. What do your scores, and the notes you made as you went along, tell you?

If you suspect that fears of abandonment fuel your unhealthy helping and giving, you may want to address this with a psychotherapist. In the meantime, can you agree it's better to have relationships with people who mainly want to have a relationship with you because they like or love *you* and not mainly because of what you give to them? How are you going to find out whom those people are unless you subject your abandonment beliefs to a test?

You may find it helpful to cultivate new relationships where you keep your generosity in check. Indeed, you'll find many people really do like, love, or respect *you*, and not just because of what you can do for them. Removing that doubt from your relationships feels good. It's healing to learn that people from your past were dead wrong when they suggested (through their words or deeds) that you weren't lovable or likeable. [53]

All that said, it's a fact that reducing your helping and giving may lead to reduced contact with some people and occasionally, it may lead to temporary or permanent relationship loss. I recognize that this stings (after all it's rejection, one of the things people most dread), and it's hurtful and disappointing. You might even grieve over the demise of the relationship. When this happens about all you can do is remind yourself that you did the right thing, it will get easier in time, and if they don't come back, you'll have more space in your life for healthier relationships.

The Use of Defense Mechanisms by Unhealthy Helpers and Givers

Unhealthy helpers and givers often display a remarkable affinity for denial and justification. Typically, they use a variety of *defense mechanisms* in the service of their helping and giving. These unconscious distortions of reality help them avoid uncomfortable thoughts and feelings about their dysfunctional helping and giving, and allow them to continue their unhealthy behavior. When unhealthy helping and giving serve unconscious needs this is even more likely.

Psychoanalysts suggest that because defense mechanisms are unconscious and serve to protect you from things you don't want to realize, you might have trouble recognizing what you're doing without psychoanalysis (therapy conducted by a psychoanalyst). However, if you're willing to take a cold hard look at yourself and ask those closest to you whether you do these things, you can probably get a handle on which of these you do. You may also feel a bit of a twinge (or cringe) when you stumble across the ones that are relevant to you.

Admitting which ones you use in the service of your ego will make it harder to let yourself get away with it.

Box 5.3 provides some examples of common defense mechanisms used by unhealthy helpers and givers.

Box 5.3 Defense Mechanisms That Serve Unhealthy Helping

Repression—*keeping unwanted thoughts and feelings out of conscious awareness, basically a type of motivated forgetting.* Example: The giver conveniently forgets how many times they have rescued or how many times the taker has failed to keep promises, pay them back, reciprocate, etc.

Rationalization—*justifying one's ideas and actions to avoid taking responsibility or to avoid change.* Example: The giver defends the recipient and their own unhealthy helping, mostly with bogus reasons and explanations.

Projection—*accusing other people of doing or feeling what they themselves actually do or think while being oblivious to the fact that it's actually themselves they're talking about; basically a "pot calling the kettle black" kind of situation.* Example: The giver accuses other people of feeling burdened by the recipient when they themselves feel this way, or accuses people of enabling the recipient when they're the biggest enablers of all.

Denial—*refusing to accept the reality of a situation because it's painful or unpleasant.* Example: Despite evidence to the contrary, the helper steadfastly rejects the idea that their helping is unhealthy, the recipient is taking advantage, or the recipient is worsening despite their help.

Compensation—*making up for one's deficiencies or deficits.* Example: The giver feels guilty about past behavior and enables and rescues in an effort to make up for past wrongs.

Idealization—*unconsciously choosing to perceive another more positively than is warranted given the evidence.* Example: The giver romanticizes a selfish, lazy taker, seeing them more positively than they deserve, and overlooking their very real faults. This leads to continued helping, as they believe the taker will soon get it together.

Altruism—*using extreme service to others as a way to deal with one's own issues.* Example: The giver focuses on taking care of the other so that they can avoid confronting their own underperformance, problems, or addiction.

Cautions When Using the Psychodynamic Approach

The psychodynamic approach offers some interesting insights into the motivations of unhealthy givers, but use it with care. In particular, remember that this creative psychological perspective is more art than science (it's impossible to prove or disprove scientifically). I also want to remind you that unhealthy helping and giving don't always come from such a dark and negative emotional place. As I've said before, there are many possible motivations and dynamics underlying unhealthy helping and giving and almost everyone eventually finds themselves in an unhealthy helping and giving situation.

Finally, I want to caution against diagnosing yourself or others with a personality disorder. Such hard-core diagnoses are best left to professionals. Exhibiting features of the personality disorders described in the PDM doesn't justify a sweeping pronouncement that someone's personality is fundamentally wacked and their behavior is pathological. Even if this chapter rings your personal bells, I wouldn't be too quick to adopt these dramatic labels or assume it's hopeless. Instead, just use any insights from the psychodynamic approach in the service of growth and change. Try to do things differently and take charge of yourself. Consider getting therapy since the emotional and childhood roots of your unhealthy helping and giving are usually best identified and dealt with in therapy with a licensed mental health provider. Also, a therapist can serve as your personal change coach.

Six

Family Influences: Learning Codependence and Bad Helping Habits

Everyone makes occasional helping and giving mistakes. Recipients sometimes surprise us by using our giving to stagnate, rather than progress. We can't always foresee that our helping and giving will become unsustainable and exceed our energetic, emotional, or material resources. Takers aren't always obvious until they take and take (a gifted manipulator-taker can fool most people, at least temporarily). A dual helping relationship can start out well only to go bad later. When helping and giving situations sour, many people get out and move on after learning a few important lessons.

But other people aren't so quick to walk away and learn their lessons. Their unhealthy helping and giving habits were forged in a family crucible and are hard to break. Dysfunctional helping and giving are well-learned behavior patterns automatically enacted in the face of a helping or giving opportunity. Growing up among masters of unhealthy giving, they learn to rescue, enable, and over-help when exposed to certain situational cues (stimulus-response). Their unhealthy helping and giving are learned behaviors. Without realizing it, they carry on a family tradition of unbalanced relationships and unsustainable giving. Some habitually over-give, accommodate, and bail others out. Before they know it, they've entered into yet another codependent relationship. Others suddenly find themselves in a specific type of dysfunctional helping and giving relationship they observed in their childhood.

This chapter explains how family dynamics and parenting may promote codependence and unhealthy helping and giving habits. It also explains how unhealthy helping and giving habits are learned, why they persist, and how to use learning theories to adopt healthier helping and giving habits.

Observational Learning: Family Helping and Giving Scripts

Unhealthy helping and giving are often family traditions handed down from one generation to another. If you're an unhealthy giver, a shake of your family tree will likely reveal other family members with similar unhealthy helping and giving patterns.

Unhealthy helping and giving may seem normal to us if we grew up in a family where it was familiar and routine. In other words, we probably learn some of our dysfunctional helping and giving through *observational learning*. Also known as *social learning*, this type of learning was identified by Albert Bandura, one of the most important psychologists of the last century. [54] The basic idea is that people often learn how to act by observing the behavior of another (a model) rather than through direct experience. For instance, research finds that parents' helping behavior, and what they say about helping, influences the helping of their children even when those children become adults. [55]

Lola, for example, recently recognized she was enabling her adult son and husband. She carried them both financially and did most of the household labor. She created numerous justifications for their irresponsibility and her over-helping. In counseling, Lola realized she was enacting the same pattern as her misery-ridden mother, who had enabled Lola's older brother and father in much the same way. Lola unknowingly replicated what she'd learned from this important childhood role model.

Research indicates children are most likely to learn behaviors from models who are powerful in their world and with whom they have a warm, nurturing relationship. Although what models do is probably more important than what they say about helping, apparently both are important. In short, if we grow up watching important adults over-help, rescue, and enable, and hear them justify their helping, then we're more likely to learn it, and do it when in similar situations. These *behavioral scripts* are usually learned and enacted without our conscious awareness. Because these patterns often repeat without awareness, therapy is sometimes necessary for identifying and breaking them.

One way to think of it is that once learned, our dysfunctional helping and giving behavior is *primed*. We're primed when our observed experience creates an association in our minds between a particular situational cue (stimulus) and a particular behavior (response) such that we're likely to behave accordingly when exposed to the cue. Due to learning, specific situations essentially activate a "program" in the brain that sets into motion a predictable behavioral sequence (the behavioral script determines the specifics). That's because this connection was learned and encoded in the brain's neural pathways.

This cognitive feature mostly serves us well since it increases cognitive efficiency. It means we don't have to spend much time thinking about what to do. Instead, we just react automatically based on learned associations, and those automatic behaviors become habit. Ironically, much of human cognition (thinking) occurs very quickly, without conscious thought. However, in the case of unhealthy helping and giving, our tendency to develop entrenched habits doesn't help us. Observing unhealthy helpers leads some of us to learn unhealthy helping associations. These prime us to repeat the mistakes of our dysfunctional helping and giving role models. While children don't usually copy behaviors from models whose behavior leads to punishing consequences, unhealthy helping and giving scripts are often learned when we're too young to understand or have access to their negative consequences. Instead, we just learn that in this situation this is what people do.

Behavior is a function of both the environment and the person. Internal personal factors (thoughts, feelings, individual biology, and established behavior patterns) interact with environmental influences to create behavior. [56] For example, children vary in how much attention they pay to their parental role models. Some children pay lots of attention to what their parents do, while others pay less attention and model from peers and other adults. To win their parents' approval, or because they strongly identify with them, some children emulate their parents while others don't. Children may pay more attention to one parent than another and learn one's behavioral scripts but not the other's (for example, children that identify as boys often pay more attention to their father's behavior than their mother's). Personality also affects how the environment affects us. For instance, a more agreeable high-A child (see Chapter 4) may be more amenable to the observational learning of helping and giving behaviors than a child that's low-A.

Although we sometimes act like reactive automatons responding to environmental triggers and acting from habit, we have consciousness and we can be creative, proactive, and reflective *if we choose to.* We have what Bandura calls "personal agency." From a cognitive psychology perspective, we may learn bad helping habits that we enact automatically but we can also choose to slow down and engage our conscious thinking processes to override our reflexive unhealthy helping habits. Cognitive psychologist Daniel Kahneman would call this switching from System 1 thinking which is automatic and reflexive, to System 2 thinking, which involves conscious, effortful thinking. [57]

You can use Box 6.1 to identify some family roots of your unhealthy helping and giving.

Box 6.1 Is Your Unhealthy Helping and Giving a Result of Intergenerational Learning?

1. Who were your helping and giving role models?
2. Which members of your family have a tendency to rescue or bail out others, or over-do for others? Who did they try to help and how?*
3. As a child or young person did you witness unhealthy helping and giving relationships similar to your own?

4. What does all this tell you about the intergenerational roots of your unhealthy helping and giving? If this is a family pattern, is it one you want to continue? Why or why not?

*Note that you may have been the beneficiary of the help or giving.

Use Box 6.2 to help you identify some healthy helping and giving role models.

Box 6.2 Identify Some Healthy Helping Role Models

The principles of observational learning suggest we can learn new behaviors vicariously, by observing the behavior of role models. In this activity, you identify some healthy helping and giving role models.

1. Who do you know that's a model of appropriate helping and giving boundaries? What can you learn from how they respond to potential helping and giving situations?
2. Who do you know that once had a problem with unhealthy helping and giving but has learned how to set appropriate boundaries? How did they do this? What can you learn from them?

Note: Al-Anon meetings and codependence support groups (CoDA groups) may be a good source of role models.

Learning Codependence From Our First Love Relationship

In the 1970s attachment theorist John Bowlby suggested that early attachments to parents influence our later relationship styles because they become "inner working models" (IWMs) of our self and others in relationships. [58] Available research indicates he was probably right. Furthermore, emotional abuse or neglect from a parent in infancy and early childhood appears to foster an insecure attachment organization that affects our later relationships. [59]

From an attachment perspective, we can learn codependence if our first primary attachment is to an under-functioning or difficult parent. Because the parent-child relationship is our first love relationship, it sets the stage for our later love relationships. If we learned the only way to connect with our difficult or emotionally neglectful parent was to suppress our own needs and wishes, and cater to theirs to receive their love, attention, and approval, then we're set up for future codependent relationships with similar types of individuals.

Attachment theory suggests that parentified children who experienced a parent's love in the context of taking care of their parent or the parent's responsibilities, are at greater risk for future codependent relationships. To them, that's what a love relationship looks like. Similarly, children with manipulative parents who convinced them to accept abuse or excessive control as love may be at greater risk for codependent relationships with difficult takers. Their love relationship template draws them to relationships where they engage in self-sacrifice to get and keep the affection of a difficult person.

Remember that relationship templates aren't set in stone. In fact, there's a good chance that the love relationship template can be overwritten by new, healthy relationship experiences. [60] We can modify our template by consciously choosing healthy over unhealthy relationships, and avoiding and ending codependent relationships. It may feel strange and unfamiliar at first, but it can become our new normal.

Raising Your Children to Be Healthy, Non-Codependent Helpers and Givers

A reader of my *Psychology Today* blog asked how to prevent her granddaughter from replicating a family pattern of codependence. Basically, I told her that to break a codependent family pattern we have to provide healthy helping role models to the youngsters in our life.

We don't want to model that good and responsible people sacrifice themselves to take care of selfish and under-functioning people. Instead, we have show them and tell them that loving someone and being a good person doesn't mean accepting imbalanced relationships and allowing others to take advantage of you. That may mean setting boundaries around our own unhealthy helping and giving so our youngsters don't bear witness to our enabling or to our relationships with abusive, selfish takers.

If we're in a codependent relationship that diverts our attention and resources away from them, we need to end it or change it. Otherwise, our children will feel unloved and unlovable which sets them up for future codependent relationships. They may also underachieve and under-function since that appears to be the route to receiving love and care from us.

Because parentification in childhood may promote codependence in adulthood, we shouldn't expect our children to assume our adult responsibilities. When we face emotional or mental health challenges, it's best to seek support from other adults, rather than from our children. Turning our non-adult children into confidantes so we can get emotional support or feel cared for may set them up for a life of finding love in relationships where their needs are sacrificed to other people's needs.

This means one of the best defenses against creating codependent offspring is to address our own codependence, addictions, mental health issues, and/or emotional challenges so that we can take care of our children's emotional and physical needs. Avoiding abusive and shame-based parenting methods is also important. Otherwise, our children learn to associate love with abuse and shame, which leads them into relationships where they're abused and shamed.

All this is necessary if we don't want our children to spend their lives seeking the love of unavailable, difficult, self-centered, addicted, or troubled people. We need to have it together enough to consistently meet *their* emotional and physical needs so that's what love looks like to them. We need to show an interest in who they are and what they like so that they cultivate identities that don't revolve around caring for under-functioning people and denying their own needs. No doubt that this is easier said than done, but a licensed family therapist or other mental health professional can help.

Our unhealthy helping and giving can affect our children in important ways so it's critical to teach them through our words and deeds that satisfying intimate relationships are equitable over time and that mutual caring and giving builds healthy intimacy. We have to teach them by talking, and through example, to step back and think it through before impulsively helping or giving. We have to get our own helping and giving house in order by using techniques from this or other books, going to support groups, or seeking professional help if needed.

Operant Learning: The Reinforcement of Unhealthy Helping and Giving

Some people don't understand why a person might over-help, enable, and rescue given how hard it is on them. But from a *behaviorist perspective* this just means that the unhealthy helping and giving has its own rewards. For instance, it can make us feel like a good person, provide excitement, enhance our social image, or reduce our anxiety (among other things). After all, if there were absolutely nothing to be gained we probably wouldn't do it.

Key to the behaviorist perspective is operant learning theory. Most often associated with psychologist B.F. Skinner (1904-1990), it's all about how the consequences that follow our behavior affect whether or not we do it again. The fundamental principle of operant conditioning is the *principle of reinforcement,* the idea that behaviors are learned based on their consequences. [61]

The bottom line, according to operant learning, is that unless a person has chocolate pudding (or some other brown substance) for brains, they must somehow benefit from their helping and giving nonsense because otherwise, they wouldn't keep doing it. The fact their behavior is habitual means it must somehow be positively or negatively reinforced. Understanding how this works is essential to *applied behavior analysis,* a behaviorist approach to personal change you'll learn about later in the chapter.

Positive reinforcement occurs when a positive consequence follows a behavior and thereby strengthens it, making it more likely to be repeated. For example, the recipient's gratitude, the attention you receive when you complain to friends about your dilemma, or the excitement that comes with crisis and rescue or giving a generous gift, can all positively reinforce dysfunctional helping and giving behavior. For those with codependent tendencies, a positive reinforcer is often intimacy. Codependents often depend on relationships with low-functioning others to feel needed, valued, competent, and close to others. These are strong reinforcing consequences for people who haven't learned other ways to get these needs met.

Another potential positive reinforcing consequence is suggested by social psychologist Robert Cialdini's *empathic-joy model of helping.* [62] [63] It proposes that some helpers experience feelings of excitement and euphoria when they help. Cialdini calls this "helper's high" and some unhealthy givers undoubtedly experience it when they rescue or give generously. According to some theorists, this helper's high has addictive qualities because it activates the same brain pleasure centers stimulated by gambling or drugs. [64] This is interesting to think about given that some people characterize codependence as an addiction.

Many of the motivations for unhealthy helping and giving discussed in this book may serve as reinforcers when viewed through the lens of operant learning theory. Box 6.3 helps you identify the positive reinforcers of your unhealthy helping and giving habits.

Box 6.3 How Is Your Unhealthy Helping and Giving Reinforced?

Directions: Place a mark in the space next to the positive reinforcers of your rescuing and enabling behavior.

____**Helper's high**

Examples: I feel a boost in my mood after helping or giving. I feel excited when I help or give.

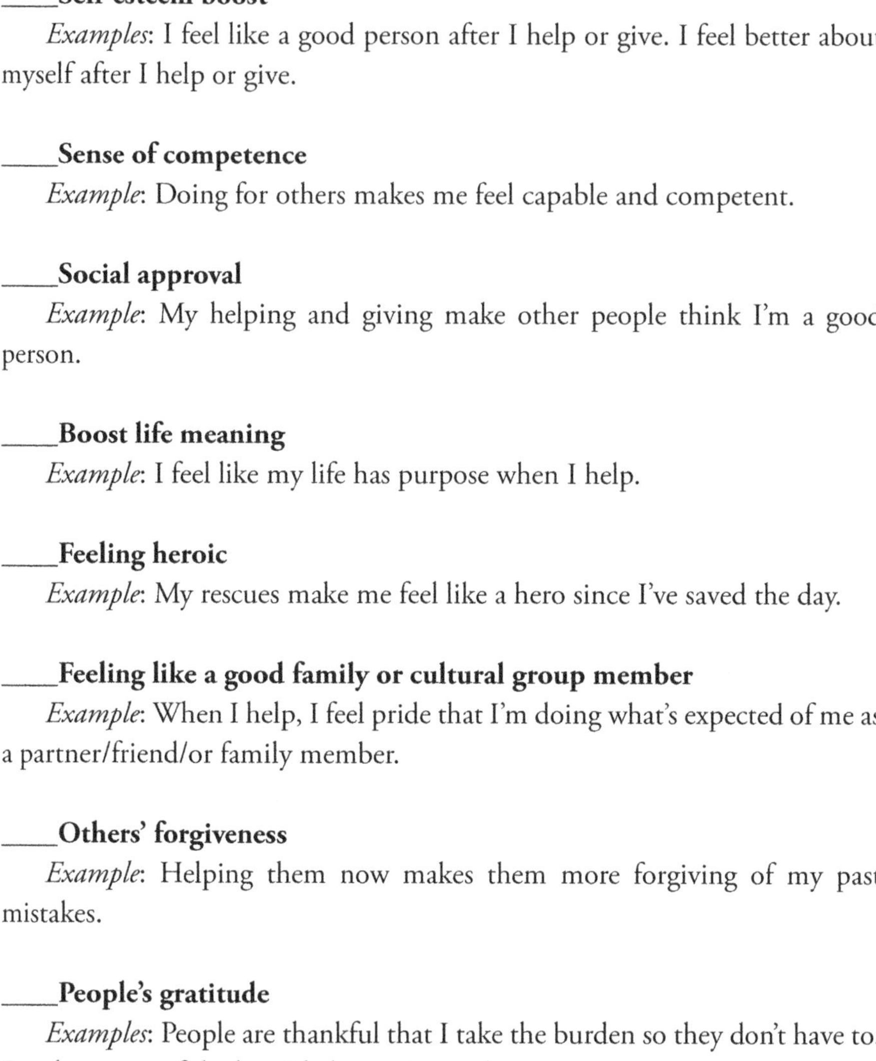

____**Self-esteem boost**

Examples: I feel like a good person after I help or give. I feel better about myself after I help or give.

____**Sense of competence**

Example: Doing for others makes me feel capable and competent.

____**Social approval**

Example: My helping and giving make other people think I'm a good person.

____**Boost life meaning**

Example: I feel like my life has purpose when I help.

____**Feeling heroic**

Example: My rescues make me feel like a hero since I've saved the day.

____**Feeling like a good family or cultural group member**

Example: When I help, I feel pride that I'm doing what's expected of me as a partner/friend/or family member.

____**Others' forgiveness**

Example: Helping them now makes them more forgiving of my past mistakes.

____**People's gratitude**

Examples: People are thankful that I take the burden so they don't have to. People are grateful when I help or give to them.

____**Relationship Closeness**

Examples: I feel very close to people when I give to them or help them. I see people I care about more than I would if I didn't help or give to them.

____ **Honeymoon**

Example: After I help another with whom I have a "rocky" relationship, there is a period of calm and pleasantness between us.

____**Excitement**

Example: I feel excited when there's some sort of crisis I can remedy.

____**Sense of Control**

Examples: Helping others means they're obligated to do what I want them to. My intervention insures that things are done how and when I think they should be done.

____**Other positive reinforcers of your behavior (describe)**

Behaviors can be positively reinforced or *negatively reinforced.* In other words, some behaviors are strengthened because they allow us to avoid or terminate negative consequences. For example, when a giver feels less guilty due to their helping, their helping is negatively reinforced because it allows them to avoid unpleasant guilt feelings. Here are some of the most common negative reinforcers of unhealthy helping and giving:

- *Repeatedly giving in to the other person's requests to avoid conflict or hassle with them.* I've heard many people say they continue in their unhealthy helping and giving because past attempts to set boundaries resulted in lots of drama. The way to avoid that drama: accept an unhealthy helping or giving arrangement. "He gets so mad if I tell him to clean up after himself or look for a job and I can't stand it when he's mad," said a mother with a 27-year old living at home. "It's just easier to let it go rather than fight with him."

- *Rescuing to reduce your empathic distress.* This is basically saving the other so you can avoid the pain of watching them flounder around trying to get it together. "I just can't stand to watch him struggle," said another parent, "It's just too painful for me."
- *Rescuing the other to avoid feeling guilty if you didn't.* Many helpers and givers say this is one of the main things holding them back from setting boundaries. They fear feeling terrible if the other fails to take care of themselves or comes to some harm they could've prevented with their help. "How would I feel if she ended up on the streets? Why I just couldn't live with myself!" said one helper of her drug-addicted sister after she gave her sister yet another "loan."
- *Continuing the unhealthy helping and giving relationship because you fear being alone and losing the relationship if you don't.* "If I didn't give him so much, I'm not sure he'd want to have a relationship with me," said one man of his boyfriend.
- *Over-helping and taking on another's problems to avoid facing your own.* By focusing on others and what they should be doing and how you can compensate for their failings, you're able to avoid dealing with your own issues. An added bonus: concentrating on others' dysfunction may make yours pale in comparison, helping you to feel good about yourself.

Negatively reinforced unhealthy helping and giving behaviors are interesting because although they allow us to avoid pain or discomfort in the short run, the result is more trouble in the long run. It's usually best to focus on the long-term benefits of setting healthy helping and giving boundaries as we ride out any short-term negative consequences. Chapters 8, 9, and 10 have tips for managing the uncomfortable feelings that sometimes accompany boundary setting.

Using Operant Learning Theory for Healthy Helping & Giving

Because we learn and repeat behaviors with positive consequences, behavioral psychologists recommend positively reinforcing the *desired* behavior.

In this case, the desired behaviors might include simply saying "No, I can't help" to another's request for a bailout, telling the other person that you have confidence in them that they can handle it themselves, not answering the phone when you see it's them, and not offering help when you aren't truly in a position to give it or it might enable another. For some, it might be cutting back on generous gifts, no longer doing others' work, or avoiding or scaling down relationships with high-maintenance, low-functioning takers.

The thing about habits though, is that once learned, they operate without conscious awareness. There is a stimulus, such as a taker in financial crisis, and we respond in our programmed way, such as giving them money. This means that once learned, you usually have to bring the habits into consciousness to modify them (switch from System 1 cognition to System 2 cognition), at least until new healthier habits are established.

The best way to do this is by tracking our behavior and having a specific plan for reinforcing the desired behaviors. Box 6.4 helps you modify your behavior with applied behavior analysis, a modern application of operant learning theory for behavior change.

Box 6.4 Modifying Your Unhealthy Helping and Giving Behavior with Applied Behavior Analysis

1. Look back at the positive reinforcers of your unhealthy helping and giving behavior identified in the Box 6.3 activity. Next to each one you identified, write down other, healthier ways to attain these positive consequences, ways that don't involve excessive rescuing, over-helping or over-giving, or enabling.
2. Take a piece of paper and make two columns. In the first column, make a very specific list of your unhealthy helping and giving behaviors (don't just name it, identify the who, what, where of it). In the

second column, make a list of what you need to say or do *instead* of your typical behaviors (once again, being very specific).

3. Looking at the list you generated of the desired behaviors, how could you strengthen (reinforce) these new, desired behaviors by following them with positive consequences? Create a plan that rewards you when you deny a rescuing impulse, withhold an urge to over-help or over-give, etc. Consider material rewards such as a small purchase, food rewards such as a favorite candy, or social or leisure-time rewards such as a visit with a friend or a few hours to relax or pursue a hobby.
4. Monitor your progress and systematically reward yourself when you replace an unhealthy helping or giving behavior with a healthy response.

Reinforcing the Dependence or Independence of Others

Sometimes our help and giving rewards and reinforces another's helplessness, dependence, or incompetence. Amber complained every time she had to find her husband's keys, rescue him when he ran out of gas, or help him finish reports for work (late due to his procrastination), but she always came through for him even though it burdened her. His behavior had relatively few negative consequences for him (other than Amber's temporary irritation and his temporary panic), and mostly positive consequences (the delay of unpleasant tasks and feeling cared for by Amber), and so it continued.

Early in the book I suggested one downside of unhealthy helping and giving is that others don't learn how to be competent, mature people when we rescue them all the time. In operant learning theory terms, unhealthy helping and giving prevents others from experiencing the negative consequences of their poor choices, and the positive consequences of more mature choices and behavior. So why would they change when your helping or giving makes it work for them?

Behavior theorists (behaviorists) point out a behavior should go away (or *extinguish*) if we withdraw positive reinforcement. However, they also emphasize that it can take a while to extinguish a behavior. This means that consistency is essential for extinguishing a habitual behavior. For example, let's say a taker overreacts to everyday life challenges and the giver reinforces this behavior by intervening and taking care of things for them. The giver decides to extinguish the taker's drama and helpless behavior by refusing to rescue them. At first, the taker regresses to get the giver back on board ("I can't do it! See how I'm falling apart! You must help me, me, me!"). This is normal. When we withdraw positive consequences and stop reinforcing their behavior, people's initial response is often to escalate it in search of the usual desired consequence. It often takes time for people to learn the behavior won't be rewarded any longer.

It takes even longer if you occasionally give in. Although it's hard, it's important you don't give in even occasionally, as this actually strengthens the undesired behavior. In essence, the person learns that although the behavior doesn't work all of the time, it works some of the time, making it worth repeating for the occasional payoff (jackpot!). Indeed, *partially reinforced* behaviors (behaviors that are reinforced part of the time) are especially resistant to eradication. If you doubt this just think about gambling and how occasional wins reinforce continued gambling despite the fact it often doesn't pay off.

Because you're dealing with a human with conscious cognition and personal agency, you can move things along more quickly by announcing your new helping and giving rules. If they persist in pushing the new boundaries, calmly tell them again, assuring them you have faith in them. This may take a while, especially if in the not-too-distant past, you violated your own helping and giving boundaries. Chapters 7 and 10 have some strategies for managing the uncomfortable thoughts and feelings that may otherwise lead you to back down. Chapter 9 discusses assertiveness skills. These are useful for dealing with those persistent, under-functioning others that refuse to get with the new program.

Many people think the way to change another person's behavior is through punishment but punishing the taker's behavior isn't particularly effective. Shaming, blaming, or yelling before, during, or after a rescue is not nearly as powerful as positively reinforcing baby steps toward the desired independent behaviors (this is called *shaping*), and making sure you don't reinforce the undesired behavior. Remember, even if you gripe about it and make them feel badly about needing your help, as long as you continue to bail them out, their unhealthy reliance on you may be positively reinforced. It's better to positively reinforce their steps in the right direction.

Punishment is also often ineffective because people often associate the punishment with the punisher instead associating it with their behavior (good old classical learning instead of good old operant learning). This leads them to dislike (or even hate) the punisher and react to the punisher in the way they react to the punishment. Punishment also frequently produces resistance and rebellion, especially in people with certain types of personalities. This is one reason why many people persist in their destructive behavior and fail to uphold agreements when helpers admonish or shame them for needing help.

Seven

The Cognitive Roots of Unhealthy Helping and Giving

This chapter is about taking charge of your head so you can respond more rationally to situations where you might help or give. As it turns out, our unhealthy helping and giving is often initiated and maintained by a variety of exaggerated thoughts. The *cognitive-behavioral perspective* helps us identify and challenge these maladaptive thoughts (*cognitions*) so we can enjoy better mental health and function more effectively.

Let's start with Diane's story. Diane felt stuck in an unhealthy helping relationship due to some stubborn but mistaken beliefs. Recognizing this was key to her change. Diane's helping horror story begins with her generous rescue of a teenager named Dylan. A friend of her son's, she knew Dylan since he was a sweet young boy. About to be released from a psychiatric facility, neither of his divorced (and low-functioning) parents was particularly interested in taking him. He called Diane from the hospital, sounding forlorn and abandoned. A bit of an empathic rescuer, Diane impulsively suggested he come live with her and her family. She made it clear that all she expected in return was that he go to school, do his homework and a few chores, and stay out of trouble. Dylan agreed.

It was a promise barely made before it was broken. Dylan was demanding, temperamental, socially inappropriate, and pitted family members against one another. He strained limited family financial resources and routinely got into trouble at school for bullying other kids and disrupting the classroom. He also failed his classes because he refused to do his homework. After a year of loving and supporting Dylan, it wasn't working out, at least not for Diane and the rest of the family.

One day I called to see how Diane was doing. She was obsessing over her failure to help Dylan. Not one to give up, and believing she was a competent decision-maker, parent, and problem-solver, she was determined to set him right. Besides, in her mind, she made a commitment to caring for him that she couldn't back away from, especially since he had nowhere else to go. These beliefs led her to feel that she had no choice other than to continue trying to save him.

I put on my cognitive-behaviorist hat, and gently questioned some of the beliefs that underpinned her feelings of distress and entrapment.

"We're stuck because he doesn't have anywhere else to go," she told me.

"Is it really true that the boy has no place to go? Really and truly true? No relatives to take him in? At one time didn't he live with his grandfather?" I asked.

"Well," she hesitated, "Yes, he does have a grandfather he could possibly live with. He lived with him before. And, if worse came to worse, he could live with his mother and stepfather in Missouri. I took him in because he convinced me that he didn't have anywhere to go but I guess he really does, although it's not ideal, and he won't like it."

I then asked, "Do you have a have a legal commitment to continue to care for him?"

"No, I don't," she admitted, "It's just that I would feel like a failure if I gave up. And I would feel so cold-hearted if I cut him loose."

"Is it really true that your inability to fix Dylan means that you're not an extremely competent, kind-hearted, and wise person with many talents?" I asked. After all, I pointed out, this boy was quite troubled and she wasn't a miracle worker, even mental health professionals had little success in helping him. I told her she gave it her best shot, but apparently her efforts couldn't undo years of parental neglect (and what appeared to be some faulty genetic wiring leading to problems with impulsiveness and emotional regulation). Perhaps it was time to accept that she couldn't turn his life around and it was time to let him go before he took her family down with him.

"But I made a commitment," she said, "I said he could live here and that we would help him. I can't go back on my word."

"I know it feels that way. You're a good person to want to honor your commitments. That's something to be proud of. But you didn't commit to this, you committed to helping someone that promised he'd go to school, take his medication, stay out of trouble, and be a contributing member of the household. You didn't sign up for this. You wouldn't have agreed to this, so is it possible that you aren't really going back on your word if you end the arrangement?"

I asked her if she could agree that giving up didn't make her a failure, or a bad person, an incompetent parent, or a person that didn't honor her commitments. Did she not do far more than most people would have? Aren't there some people that we can't help? Weren't there extenuating circumstances that made it okay to back away from this helping situation?

"Yes, I suppose that's true" she said laughing, "I really did do my best but you're right, I'm not a miracle worker!" She later reported that this was a moment of clarity for her and she strengthened her new counter-belief (that supported letting him go rather than sticking it out) by writing an affirmation on a piece of paper and posting it on her refrigerator where she looked at it daily. "I'm pretty great, but I'm not a f*cking miracle worker," it said. The boy went to live with his grandfather and the topsy-turvy household was righted once Dylan's chaotic influence was removed.

Like many people, once Diane made a commitment to rescue and help, she developed strong beliefs to rationalize and justify her choice. These beliefs led to *helping entrapment*. As I said earlier in the book, once you generate justifications for your helpfully-intended intervention, these drive continued intervention. After all, continuing to help is consistent with these reasons while terminating your helping isn't. Once we've committed to something and justified it, justifying similar actions is easy. If you justified one act of helping, it may feel contradictory to decline a similar, later request or need for help (and remember, we tend to experience cognitive dissonance when we behave inconsistently). Because Diane's help required significant time, effort, and expense, *dissonance due to effort* contributed to her escalating commitment. She freely chose to invest time, energy, and money into a cause (in this case Dylan), only to find it didn't have the intended results. She hung in there, hoping it would all eventually pay off so she wouldn't feel foolish, lose her investment, and have to face that she couldn't help Dylan after all.

As far as this chapter is concerned, Diane's story is important because it illustrates that we can get stuck in an unhealthy helping relationship due to a series of faulty beliefs originating in our initial efforts to justify our choice to help. For a time, Diane operated according to the false belief she had no choice but to care for Dylan because he had no place else to go. She falsely believed she had no choice but to honor her commitment, and that she'd be a bad and incompetent person if she ended the arrangement. The story also demonstrates another important point of this chapter: if you're willing to identify and challenge the irrational and extreme thoughts that underpin your unhealthy helping or giving commitment, then your behavior (and your feelings) can also change.

The Basics of the Cognitive-Behavioral Perspective

Examining unhealthy helping and giving through the lens of the *cognitive-behavioral perspective* is the focus of this chapter. Today, cognitive behavioral therapies are some of the most popular and effective psychological treatment models available. Often associated with psychologist Albert Ellis and psychiatrists David Burns and Aaron Beck, the basic idea is that many maladaptive (problem) behaviors arise from faulty thoughts and beliefs that lead to our feelings and behavior. Techniques from *cognitive behavior therapy (CBT)* are useful for addressing the cognitive roots of unhealthy helping and giving.

CBT focuses on *self-talk* as the key to what you feel and what you do. Self-talk is just what it sounds like; it's what you tell yourself. For example, many people who enable and rescue see someone struggling and automatically think things like, "I must take responsibility for helping this person or I am a bad person, parent, friend, sibling, manager, or coworker," or, "If I don't give, the other will be mad at me and reject me and I couldn't stand that." The big idea here is that these types of exaggerated thoughts are often the forerunners of unhealthy helping and giving.

Imagine a situation where you believe the other person faces disaster unless you help. As a consequence, you feel distressed about the other's situation and guilty at the thought of not helping, and so you see it as your duty to rescue. Now imagine that someone else witnesses the same situation but this person doesn't interpret it as a calamity but rather as a character-and-skill building experience for the other that they'll survive and learn from. Although they believe they could temporarily ease the other's burden if they intervened, they don't believe that it's their duty to solve this person's problem, nor do they believe their help would benefit the other in the long run. Consequently, they do not feel extremely upset by the situation nor do they rescue. Once again, the point is that *what you think and what you tell yourself play a critical role in what you do.*

Now on the face of it this does not seem particularly revelatory. However, when you consider two other important things about this approach its significance becomes apparent. The first thing is that *some of the beliefs leading to our unhealthy helping (and our suffering around it) may be faulty and even blatantly irrational* once we think about them (this approach is about thinking about our thoughts!). To paraphrase Albert Ellis, we create some of our own needless misery through our "crooked" thinking. The second thing is that this has implications for change—*we can change our behavior and our feelings by challenging and changing what we say to ourselves* and *by challenging and changing what we think about "activating events."* That's what this chapter is about.

Common Irrational Beliefs Underlying Unhealthy Helping and Giving

To change your feelings and behavior, you first have to learn what irrational beliefs are tripping you up so I want to give you an idea of the types of things helpers and givers think and believe that get them into trouble. We'll start off with some ideas from Albert Ellis (who lived from 1913-2007). Ellis identified a number of extreme and irrational beliefs that create "emotional disturbance."[65] Some of these are quite relevant to unhealthy helping and giving.

Ellis, for example, suggested that one irrational belief is that *other people's "disturbances" are horrible" and we must feel very upset by them*. Not only does this belief mean we experience excessive distress in regards to others' predicaments, but it makes us feel compelled to intervene, and distraught when our efforts don't pay off as intended. For example, people in long-term unhealthy helping and giving relationships often experience significant worry and anxiety about the other's repeated irresponsibility, poor living conditions, or bad behavior so they keep intervening. Some have difficulty living and enjoying their own life due to the distress they experience over another's poor functioning.

However, as Ellis points out, we're limited in our power to change others and their situations (though we do have the power to change ourselves!). As hard as it may be for us to believe, they may even be okay with their situation and the way they're living their life. So, *if available evidence suggests we can't help them to change or they don't want to change, then it's time to accept reality and stop being so horrified by their life and the failure of our rescues to alter them.* Do your best to help, he says, but if it's not working, accept what you can't change and start living your life. [66] This is what Diane did to get her life back and what I try to practice as well.

According to Ellis, another common irrational belief leading to our emotional disturbance is that *other people must like and approve of us all the time and it'll be just awful if they don't.* Many givers are people-pleasers with a low tolerance for others' displeasure with them. Believing you must always please everyone sets you up for unhealthy rescuing, over-helping, and enabling. This includes saying such things to yourself as, "If I don't help, the other will be really mad at me, and it will be just awful, and I won't be able stand it!" (This statement also illustrates what Ellis calls *awfulizing* and *can't-stand-itis.*) However, as I suggested in an earlier chapter, sometimes the best thing to do is to stand it for a while. If you give others a chance to solve their own problems you'll often find that your action isn't really needed. This also prevents you from overreacting due to your initial strong, empathic response.

If you really believe that you can't live with others' occasional unhappiness with you and your boundaries, you're destined to fall down the rabbit-hole of dysfunctional helping and giving relationships. Ellis rightly argues it's ridiculous to believe that we can never displease others or tolerate their displeasure. Of course you can stand other people getting mad or irritated with you. You might not like it, but you can stand it. After all, while it's certainly unpleasant to have someone unhappy with you it's rarely fatal.

Anyways, as noted previously, helping or giving to someone doesn't guarantee they won't get mad at you nor does it guarantee they'll always think you're perfect and wonderful (see the Chapter 3 discussion of negative reactions to our help and gifts). It's also just plain old irrational to keep helping and giving so someone won't be mad at you, especially since their anger is likely to be short-lived, and the relationship usually survives (as long as there was more to it than your helping them).

One feature of the irrational thoughts described above is what Ellis calls *musterbation.* When we "musterbate," we "must ourselves" into emotional distress with extreme and absolutist declarations we adhere to like a sacred vow. Those with long-standing unhealthy helping and giving patterns are typically musterbation masters who "must" and "should" themselves into all kinds of dysfunctional thoughts and behaviors. Here are some typical unhealthy helping and giving "musterbations":

- I must be extremely self-sacrificing and put other's needs above my own, or I'm not a good person.
- Being a good mother/father/friend/sibling/co-worker/etc. means I must help or give.
- I must rescue others or they will not love me (or like me).
- To receive people's approval, I must always please them.
- I must say, "yes," to all requests for assistance or others will get mad at me and it'll be awful.
- I must rescue the other or they'll face ruin and it'll be my fault and I'll feel horribly guilty and I won't be able to stand it.
- I must continue to help or give because it's my duty.

- The other person must do what I think they should do because I'm helping them.
- The other must show their gratitude for my help in the ways that I expect or I must feel hurt and victimized.

Ellis also says it's irrational to insist that *our emotional distress is mainly externally caused and we have little or no ability to change our feelings and behavior.* For example, you may claim that you have no choice but to be horribly distressed by the other's self-imposed disasters and that means you have no choice other than to help. But the truth is that you do have choices. You can choose how you interpret the other's situation, which will affect how you feel, and what you do (more on how to do this later). Although it won't necessarily be easy to change your thoughts, feelings, and behavior, according to Ellis, it is a gross exaggeration to suggest that you cannot. Put it this way, you don't have to let your own thinking bully you into unhealthy helping and giving.

Ellis recommends that people suffering from irrational thinking take ten minutes a day to "actively and vigorously" challenge their own thinking using the DIBS technique (Dispute Irrational Beliefs and Surrender). Box 7.1 shows you how to use the DIBS method to challenge your irrational helping and giving thoughts and beliefs.

Box 7.1 Disputing and Surrendering Your Irrational Helping and Giving Beliefs

Part I. Review the preceding material and identify a self-defeating irrational belief you want to dispute and surrender.

Part II. Now strenuously argue with it by answering the questions below. Really give it a hard time, challenging any "awfulizing" and "can't-stand-itis" while creating new beliefs promoting self-acceptance. Then, write down or video-record your responses and review until the irrational belief is powerless.

A. What evidence exists of the falseness of this belief?
B. Is there any evidence the belief is true?
C. What is the worst that could happen if the belief is true, and in all honesty, could I survive and prosper despite that?
D. What good things could happen if the extreme thought were true?

Example:
What is the irrational belief underlying my unhealthy helping or giving?
"I must be self-sacrificing and rescue others or I'm not a good person and I will be rejected."

What is my evidence that the belief is false?
"I love people that aren't completely self-sacrificing and think they're still good people, so I have proof that I can be loved even if I have helping and giving boundaries."

"Even if I do not completely sacrifice myself for others, I am still a caring, giving, honest person—this makes me a good person and lovable even if I sometimes choose not to bail out others."

"Some people that do not know of my rescues think I am a good person for other reasons."

What is my evidence that this belief is true?
"I only have a little evidence. The last time I tried to say 'no' to a rescue, he said that I was heartless. I didn't hear from him for a week but I have to admit it wasn't that bad, I got through it, and he did come back."

What are the worst things that could happen to me if my extreme thought is true?
"I will feel bad that people don't like me."
"I will lose a relationship."

Could I survive it were it to happen?
"Yes, although I would prefer that people wouldn't reject me if I didn't rescue them, I could survive it."

What good things could happen if my extreme thought comes true?

"I'll discover who cares enough about me that they won't reject me if I say "no."

"I'll have the opportunity to develop healthy relationships with people who like me for reasons other than what I do for them."

"I'll have more time and more money."

"S/he will become more independent."

Common Unhealthy Helping and Giving Mindtraps

As the cognitive-behavioral perspective developed, the terminology changed from *irrational beliefs* to *self-defeating thoughts* (*mindtraps*) and the list grew.[67] Here are some common mindtraps I apply to unhealthy helping and giving:

Mindtrap 1: Catastrophizing (also known as fortune-telling). Are you a person that immediately jumps to the worst possible conclusion about someone's predicament? Do you assume that your intervention is necessary to prevent imminent disaster? Do you think things like, "Without my intervention the other will end up dead, broke, homeless, in jail, fired"? Has this type of thinking led you to impulsive rescuing and giving? Predicting worst-case scenarios leads to anxiety and panic and compels us to intervene. And most of the time, our fears are overblown.

Mindtrap 2: Mind-reading. Do you act like a mind reader, assuming people will think badly of you if you don't continue to give at such a high level? Do you think things like, "If I don't help or give, other people will think I am bad or selfish" or, "If I don't help or give, they will be very angry with me and I won't be able to stand it"? People prone to unhealthy helping and giving often falsely assume that other people will react negatively if they don't help or give or exaggerate others' negative reactions. They anticipate extreme negative reactions and judgment if they don't help or give. That induces them to give and keep on giving.

Mindtrap 3: All-Or-None Thinking. Are you like many unhealthy helpers and givers who are black-and-white thinkers whose absolutist proclamations lead them astray? Do you look at situations and people as completely right or wrong, good or bad? Do you think things like, "If I don't help, it means I'm selfish," "I love them so I *have* to give them another chance," "I said I'd help and I *can't* go back on my word," or "I *have* to help them, they're family"? All-or-none thinking can lock us into unhealthy helping and giving by making us think we have no choice but to help or give.

Mindtrap #4: Personalization. Do you feel compelled to help or give because you think someone's negative behavior or circumstances are somehow your fault and therefore your responsibility? Do you say things to yourself like, "If I was a better parent, teacher, spouse, sibling, manager (or whatever), they wouldn't be like this, therefore, I'm responsible for rescuing them"? As cognitive behavioral therapy expert David Burns says, personalization often involves confusing having an influence on others with having control over what those others do.

Mindtrap #5: Emotional Reasoning. Do you use your emotions as evidence of facts? For example, do you feel distress and alarm over another's predicament and automatically think you must intervene? Truthfully, facts are sometimes different from feelings and not all feelings should be acted upon. For example, you feel distress and alarm over another's predicament and assume this means you must rescue, when if you just settled down a bit, you'd realize this isn't the best thing to do.

Mindtrap #6: Shoulding. Are you a duty-bound person that "shoulds" yourself into carrying the loads of others? Do you think things like, "I *should* be giving and selfless" and "I *should* sacrifice my time/energy/resources if I am a good spouse/parent/coworker/friend/person"? These are basically the same thing as what Ellis calls "mustabatory thinking" and for unhealthy helpers and givers usually include thoughts like "I should (must) put others' needs above my own." Some of these cognitions arise when we define our role of good family member, intimate partner, or close friend role as requiring the provision of assistance. These beliefs often translate into absolutist declarations that preclude appropriate boundary setting (e.g., "I *should* do this for them if I'm a good ________.").

Irrational beliefs often assume a life of their own, safely protected from challenge in our fortress-like heads. They're what we believe and that's that, end of discussion. But doggedly holding on to our faulty thinking only promotes more of the same unhealthy helping and giving that are so problematic for us.

Unhealthy helpers and givers usually benefit from recognizing the extreme and over blown cognitions that fuel their unhealthy helping and giving. This is a necessary first step for change according to the cognitive behavioral approach. Box 7.2 provides an exercise to help you identify the irrational beliefs and thinking traps that apply to you.

Box 7.2 Identify the Mindtraps That Lead To Your Unhealthy Helping and Giving

Directions: Place a check next to the mindtraps below that apply to your unhealthy helping and giving and write down personal examples next to those that apply to you. If you have trouble with this, think about your most recent bailout, rescue, or over-giving experience and ask yourself, "What did I tell myself that made me feel that I had to help or give? Why did I feel that I couldn't say 'no'?"

____1. Fortune-telling or catastrophizing (Example: "If I don't help, the consequences will be awful.")

____2. Mind-reading (Example: "If don't help, other people will think badly of me or respond negatively and I won't be able to handle it.")

____3. All-or-none thinking (Example: "Good parents always help their children.")

____4. Personalization (Example: "It's my fault they need help so I'm responsible for helping.")

____5. Emotional Reasoning (Example: "I'm upset by their predicament so this means my action is necessary.")

____6. Shoulding and Musting (Example: "Being a good person means I should always put others' needs above my own.")

Counteracting Irrational Beliefs and Mindtraps

After identifying the relevant mindtraps, the antidote is to question and challenge them (time again to switch to Cognitive System 2!). The basic idea is to let some rationality in rather than to stubbornly cling to maladaptive thoughts and beliefs. Cognitive behavior therapists like David Burns recommend we:

- Examine the evidence for our faulty beliefs
- Ask others whether our beliefs are realistic
- Do an "experiment" to test the accuracy of our negative thoughts
- Be compassionate towards ourselves as we would a friend
- Evaluate things in "shades of gray" instead of in all-or-none terms
- Consider whether we're truly at fault before assuming responsibility for others
- Substitute less emotionally loaded language for "should statements"

Taking these recommendations into account, here are some suggestions for challenging the irrational beliefs and mindtraps common to unhealthy givers.

To challenge the *irrational belief that you must please others at all times to avoid disapproval* ask yourself: Is it true that others' disapproval is so unbearable that I must sacrifice myself to reduce the possibility they'll be unhappy with me? *Or* is the truth that I can survive others' displeasure with me if I determine my help or giving isn't really necessary or won't be best in the long run? Does rescuing and enabling really protect me from experiencing the disapproval of others? Isn't it true people have gotten mad or irritated with me despite or even because of my attempts to help or give to them?

Oppose the *irrational belief that you can't change your beliefs and behaviors* by considering this: Am I willing to swear on a stack of my favorite religious text that I can't change my unhealthy helping or giving because it's completely due to forces beyond my control? *Or* can I admit that I can change my harmful helping beliefs and behaviors if I really want to?

Dispute the *irrational belief that you have the power to solve others' unmanageable problems* by thinking about this: Although your good intentions are powerful stuff (God bless your kind heart!), are you really so gifted (or omnipotent) that it's realistic to expect your efforts can solve another's problems when there's proof those problems are big and complicated, they're not ready for change, and your efforts aren't working? Is it fair to consider yourself a failure if you back away from trying to fix them or their problems? What would you say to a friend in this situation? Would you support them in backing off from their well-intended, but obviously ineffective or self-destructive helping and giving?

Counteract a *personalization mindtrap* by asking yourself: Is it really true at this point in time that I'm responsible for the other person's misfortune and for fixing it? *Or* is it true that they should bear this responsibility for themselves? Even if I bear some responsibility, what are the other factors (including the other person's choices) that played a role? What do people I trust say about my responsibility for the other's problem—why should I believe my distorted thoughts instead of them?

Contemplate the following to challenge an *all-or-none thinking mindtrap*: Is it a fact that you're a bad person if you reel in your helping or giving and a good person if you don't? *Or* is it true you can set boundaries around your helping and giving and still be a good person? How can good helping and giving boundaries be consistent with being a good person? Is it always the right thing to help or give and the wrong thing not to?

Considering these questions can challenge a *mind-reading mindtrap*: Do you know beyond a shadow of a doubt that other people will think you're bad if you don't rescue or enable, or good if you do? Can you check this out with people that you respect? Do you know for a fact that others will be incredibly mad at you (rather than accepting it, or merely being irked with you) if you don't help? Are you willing to give it a try and find out?

Challenge a *catastrophizing or fortune-telling mindtrap* with the following: Thinking about your rescues, is it really and truly true (not just rationalizing-your-past actions-true) that were it not for your help, the other couldn't handle the situation or disaster would've occurred?

You can counter an *emotional reasoning mindtrap* by answering these questions: Can you say with certainty that your emotional reactions to others' predicaments are always or even mostly right and rarely, if ever, mislead you into unnecessary or harmful helping or giving? Be honest: does your empathy ever lead you astray such that you impulsively intervene without considering the costs to yourself and others, only to regret it later?

Finally, you can challenge *should statements* and *mustabatory thinking* with these questions: Is it possible that your shoulding and musting are a bit extreme? Can you soften your should statements so they're less harsh and more reasonable? Are you holding yourself to standards that you don't hold others to? For example, instead of saying "I should be selfless and sacrifice myself for others" perhaps you can say, "It's generally good to help others but there are times when it's all right not to." "I must help or I am a bad person," can be softened to, "Being a helpful, giving person is part of what makes me a good person but there are times when being a good person means not intervening to solve another's problems."

Box 7.3 helps you apply these strategies to your situation.

Box 7.3 Escaping Mindtraps with Cognitive Behavior Therapy Techniques

Now that you see how this is done, look back at your personal mind traps from Box 7.2 and then:

1. Ask yourself, "Is there really good evidence for the beliefs underlying my helping, or are they in fact, exaggerations?"
2. Use the Challenging Mindtraps section above to substitute a more realistic, balanced, and positive thought for each extreme belief you identified (this is called *positive reframing*). Then, practice, practice, practice. Learn to catch yourself when you're falling into mindtrap quicksand and pull yourself out with a rational counter-thought.
3. Check out your self-defeating beliefs with a trusted, emotionally mature advisor—do they agree that these are reasonable things to think and act on?
4. Do some experiments to test your extreme beliefs. Try saying no to rescuing in all but the grimmest of situations. Try helping and giving without exceeding you what you can really afford energetically and materially. See that everyone survives.

Identifying and challenging the maladaptive thinking underlying unhealthy helping and giving is often important for personal change. When this is a new way of thinking and doing, a CBT therapist can help you recognize and dispute your personal mindtraps. Cognitive behavior therapy is even more powerful when combined with some exploration of the origins of your bent thinking (see earlier chapters or a therapist for assistance).

Eight

How Culture and Gender Influence Unhealthy Helping and Giving

Like many human behaviors, helping and giving are influenced by cultural norms and roles. Indeed, most cultures have norms and values encouraging helping and giving to others. Benevolence and concern for others are common religious themes. Self-sacrificing saints, martyrs, and holy people are a feature of many religious traditions. Spiritual and religious perspectives that perceive God as a nurturing, caring friend—or an enlightened, compassionate Spirit within—foster a compassionate ideal self that prescribes forgiveness, volunteerism, and aid to others. [68] Cultural values encouraging helping and giving are embedded in many folktales, legends, religious parables, and proverbs.

The Old Testament of the Bible, a sacred text of both Christians and Jews says, "You should love your neighbor as yourself" (Leviticus 19:18) and in the New Testament it says, "Let no one seek their own good, but the good of their neighbor (1 Corinthians 10.24).

The Koran, the sacred text of Islam says, "Surely they who believe and do good deeds and keep up prayer and pay the poor-rate shall have their reward from their Lord, and they shall have no fear, nor shall they grieve" (2:227).

A Buddhist saying goes, "If you light a lamp for somebody, it will also brighten your path."

A Chinese proverb says, "If you want happiness for an hour, take a nap. If you want happiness for a day, go fishing. If you want happiness for a year, inherit a fortune. If you want happiness for a lifetime, help somebody."

A Hindu text, the Bhagavad Gita (3.10-26), says, "The ignorant work for their own profit, the wise work for the welfare of the world, without thought to themselves. Perform all work carefully, guided by compassion."

This chapter considers the role of gender and culture in unhealthy helping and giving. For some people, this is another important piece of their unhealthy helping and giving puzzle. The way they understand and identify with their gender or culture promotes unhealthy self-sacrifice and martyrdom for others. They go overboard when it comes to enacting cultural values that emphasize taking care of others, especially family members. They have trouble telling the difference between excessive caretaking and normal nurturing. Their dedication to others is such that their own individual identity and needs are neglected.

Considering cultural influences on helping behavior also helps us better understand and respect others' helping and giving choices. It's important to recognize that what's considered unhealthy helping and giving may vary based on culture. For example, in many East Asian cultures there are strong cultural values of family loyalty and filial piety. These values call for giving up individual desires for the sake of one's parents and family. Contrast that with many Euro American cultures where the individual comes first and many people feel little responsibility to care for parents or other family members. Before criticizing or judging someone's helping or giving or calling them codependent, it's good to *contextualize* it by considering cultural influences.

Culture and Unhealthy Helping and Giving

Although social scientists define culture in different ways, the basic idea common to most definitions is that culture represents the socially transmitted beliefs, values, and practices shared by a group. Our cultures tell us what to value, and what we should do (*prescriptive norms*) and shouldn't do (*proscriptive norms*). We are often so immersed in our cultures that we think of culture as belonging to other groups and people, but we are all products of our culture.

Although a lot of people think of culture as referring to the practices and values of different ethnic groups or nationalities, it's more accurate to think of culture broadly. Individuals operate within multiple, often overlapping cultures. As social psychologist Bernice Lott once said, we're all multicultural beings. For example, family culture, religious culture, gender culture, friendship group culture, leisure-time/hobby culture, team culture, cohort (age group) culture, and national and ethnic cultures can all influence our attitudes, beliefs, and behaviors. All of these cultures may have norms which specify who to help and give to, when, and how much to help and give.

Cultures vary in how much they emphasize benevolence and service to others and whether helping others is cast as heroic or virtuous. This may affect whether we make an initial offer of help and how much dissonance we experience when we consider withdrawing it. For example, Catherine, a devout Roman Catholic woman, modeled herself after Jesus' mother (the selfless Mary) and after the numerous Catholic women saints that sacrificed themselves for others. Believing that her religion prescribed self-sacrifice for others' benefit, she was prone to over-helping and enabling in her effort to be a good Catholic woman. Non-Catholic Christians may also struggle to temper the conceptions of Christian love and service that can lead to unhealthy helping and giving. Christian codependency groups focus on helping people honor the call to "love thy neighbor" and give selflessly to others without sacrificing their own well being in the process.

Collectivists, Individualists and Unhealthy Helping and Giving

Whether we identify with a culture that's collectivistic or individualistic may also make a difference.

Collectivists are less individualistic in their thinking and more likely to make decisions with the collective in mind. Priority is placed on the group rather than the individual and there's some expectation that individuals share their resources with other group members. Helping other group members is seen as a duty. Harmony and keeping the group together is prioritized, which sometimes means avoiding conflict and disagreement. People with collectivist values may find it more challenging to balance their need to be a good family member with their individual needs than people with individualist values. Social psychologists like Hazel Markus and Shinobu Kitayama say that people from collectivist cultures often have an *interdependent self.* [69]

In contrast, individualistic cultures place a premium on thinking about and acting on your own behalf. People from individualistic cultures get more of their self-esteem and pride from personal talents and achievements than they do from pride in being a good member of their group (they have an *independent self*). They are more oriented towards personal gain than what benefits the group. [70]

When it comes to helping and giving, collectivism and harmony values may be especially important because they likely influence feelings of social responsibility and reactions to dependency. Because people from collectivist cultures get more of their self-esteem and pride from being a loyal family member and cultural group member, they often conform more to group norms suggesting that one should take care of other group members, even if this requires personal sacrifice.

In a study comparing Taiwanese and American college students, Shih-Hua Chang found independent/individualistic cultural orientations were negatively related to codependency and interdependent/collectivistic cultural orientations were positively related to codependency. In other words, individualism is associated with reduced codependency and collectivism is associated with increased codependency. She also found that in comparison to college students in the United States, college students in Taiwan tended to be more interdependent/collectivistic and had significantly higher levels of codependency than their American counterparts. [71]

Cultural Bias and Codependence

Some cultural value orientations may promote unhealthy helping and giving more than others. But our values may also influence what we perceive as unhealthy helping and giving. Codependence in particular is sometimes criticized as a value-laden notion arising from Euro American individualistic values. For instance, social workers Jaime Inclan and Miguel Hernandez note the Hispanic cultural value of *familism* may promote putting family members' needs ahead of one's own and this isn't necessarily evidence of codependence. Likewise, common codependent treatments reflecting Anglo individualist values aren't always a good fit for those operating from more collectivist family value systems. Pushing people to label living their family values as codependence, and encouraging them to separate from unhealthy family members, is often both culturally insensitive and unproductive. [72]

This is also something to think about because intimate relationships between people from different ethno-cultural groups are increasingly common. [73] Divergent cultural ideas regarding helping and giving can give rise to culture clashes and relationship conflict. Givers from collectivist cultures may not be near as bothered by family members' dependence on them as people from individualistic cultures might expect. This is probably because the line between healthy and unhealthy helping and giving is fuzzier when your culture strongly promotes taking care of your fellow group members, sharing resources, and acting on behalf of the social unit (for example, the family). To the individualist it may look like unhealthy helping or giving, but to the collectivist it looks like being a good family member, and something they're expected and obligated to do.

This was an ongoing issue between Arminda, a Filopino American woman, and her live-in boyfriend, the Euro American Erik. They often clashed over Arminda sending money to her relatives in the Philippines. To Arminda this was just what you do, she could not see why it was a problem. To Erik, this created unnecessary financial strain and dependence and he resented it.

Of course this isn't to say that collectivists don't engage in unhealthy helping and giving or that they're never codependent. When helping or giving enables someone's immaturity, irresponsibility or poor life skills, requires lying or deception, is unsustainable given your energetic or financial resources, prevents someone from getting needed professional care, etc., it's still problematic.

Givers from collectivist cultures sometimes realize this but their boundary-setting ambivalence is magnified by their values. Those operating from more individualistic values should appreciate this. For example, withdrawing help or refusing to participate in an enabling chain may be experienced as a betrayal of family or cultural norms, leading to disapproval and conflict with friends or family. Likewise, collectivists should appreciate that this type of resource-sharing with family members may be unfamiliar and uncomfortable to their individualist-cultured partner.

To respect one's another's cultures, partners may need to share their differing cultural orientations towards giving (*intercultural exploration*). Once empathy for one another's perspectives is achieved, it's easier to meet somewhere in the middle. There is, after all, merit in helping one's family as well as merit in protecting one's limited resources, or sharing them very selectively. If such agreements are hard to work out, couples counseling might help. A good couples counselor can teach a couple how to craft cooperative solutions with little drama.

Gender and Unhealthy Helping and Giving

The gender norms and roles prescribed by traditional femininity and traditional masculinity promote unhealthy helping and giving in some people. For example, from an early age many Americans are exposed to cultural messages suggesting that heroic rescue and financial responsibility for others are stereotypically masculine. Meanwhile, they're told self-sacrificing caregiving and nurturing are stereotypically feminine. Internalizing (accepting) these cultural messages may put men and women at risk for different forms of unhealthy helping and giving.

Traditional Women's Roles and Unhealthy Helping and Giving

Compared to men, women score slightly higher on measures of prosocial motivations like social responsibility, other-centered empathy, and perspective taking (though it's important to remember that there's lots of individual variation and this may not be true of a particular man or a particular woman). Women also view empathic skills as more important to their self-concept and this affects their motivation to behave empathically. [74]

The social constructionist view of gender lays at least some of these differences at the doorstep of gender stereotypes, gender norms, and gender roles. Traditional gender stereotypes (beliefs about how males and females differ) suggest girls and women are naturally other-centered caregivers. Gender norms (social expectations based on gender) prescribe they be considerate, nice, and sweet. Traditional feminine roles such as wife, mother, daughter (and daughter-in-law), direct women to take care of children, husbands, and elderly family members. Their job as women is to make other people's lives easier by doing things for them, and to care for dependent loved ones; they provide *care labor*. All over the world, women are the ones expected to provide the majority of care labor. Even outside the home, women are most often found in service occupations, particularly clerical and retail jobs, and in professional caregiving jobs. Caring for others, and accommodating others, in and outside of the home, is often designated as "women's work."

In some cultures, selfless service to others is a defining feature of the good woman. For example, in many religious traditions, especially those that are fundamentalist, a woman's self-sacrifice on behalf of her family is cast as spiritual service to God. [75] Women may feel guilty or unnatural if they rebel against the role prescribed to them. Women, who accept these conventional gender norms and believe other people will judge them based on their conformity to these norms, may be more susceptible to unhealthy helping and giving.

Think about it this way: In an effort to demonstrate she's a good woman as defined by her culture, a woman may do too much for others, leading to others' dependence and poor life skills. She may also experience dissonance should she stop; not doing for others contradicts who she is as a woman. Setting boundaries can create internal conflict as it's at odds with the gender role expectation that she selflessly provide unconditional love and support to those she cares about.

Women may also be predisposed to unhealthy helping and giving if their culture (or subculture) discourages women's assertiveness. For example, historically in the United States, women experienced social pressure to passively serve others, to remain unassertive, to be nice, and to stay "sweet." Many women feared deviating from these norms lest they be considered by others to be a poor wife, mother, or woman. In some American subcultures, these norms persist.

Traditional gender socialization routinely promotes empathy and caregiving skills in girls in preparation for their role as wives and mothers. Meanwhile, boys are directed to activities that develop their more *agentic* qualities. They receive more social approval for being competitive and aggressive, rather than other-centered and sensitive to the needs of others.

Thinking about all that, some feminists suggest that much of the behavior and traits identified as codependent are culturally approved and encouraged for women. After all, sensitivity and other-centeredness are hallmarks of traditional femininity. They say many codependent-appearing women are just conforming to traditional feminine gender roles prescribing self-sacrifice on behalf of others. Women aren't emotionally or psychologically sick for following this cultural prescription, they're just trying to be good women in gender unequal societies where women are expected to subordinate their needs to others. [76] For example, a 2008 study by Mexican psychologist Gloria Noriega and her colleagues found that Mexican women who followed a traditional feminine "submission script" requiring self-sacrifice on behalf of their husbands and families, were almost eight times more likely than other Mexican women to score high on a measure of codependence. [77]

I know in my life, my internalization of traditional gender norms contributed to my martyr-like self-sacrifice for others. For the first half of my life, I lived in a culture where a woman's primary role was to serve others. Heterosexual marriage, which included a lifetime of service to others (in the form of cooking, cleaning, husband-care, childcare, and eldercare) was supposed to be the primary goal of every girl, and women were judged based on their conformity to this traditional gender role. Good women were passive, uncomplaining, and nice while assertive women were nags, bitches or "trying to act like men."

Indeed, I would say that internalizating traditional gender scripts prescribing devoted service to one's husband contributed to the end of my first marriage over twenty years ago. Although I violated my traditional gender role by developing a professional career and being a breadwinner, I tried to make up for it by simultaneously being a traditional wife and mother. I did the majority of housework, yardwork, home maintenance, childcare, cooking, shopping, holiday preparation, and financial management, while I worked full-time.

After ten years of of devoted service, I came to resent his freedom and leisure time and I disrespected him due to his incompetence (which I enabled). I also believed that he didn't really care about me since I was clearly overburdened and he was oblivious to my struggle. Our marriage suffered and while it was partly his fault (he did me some major wrong, best to leave it at that!), it was also mine. My efforts to simultaneously succeed as a traditional wife and mother and a high-performing professor, along with my reluctance to assert myself due to fear of being labeled a bitch by my husband and his friends, was a set up for my over-giving, exhaustion, and eventual resentment. We ended up divorcing.

It's now clear to me that in my role of wife and mother I confused the healthy nurturing of others with self-denial and martyrdom and my personality traits and childhood made this more likely. But it's also apparent to me that such self-sacrifice isn't the exclusive domain of women. In fact, most studies find small or no differences between men and women on codependence measures. [78] Some studies even find that men score higher on codependence than women. [79]

Although women's unhealthy giving can stem from over-enacting the other-centered caretaking aspect of the traditional female gender role, the data doesn't support the idea that women are significantly more likely to be codependent than men. What it does support is the idea that self-denying and self-sacrificing puts us at greater risk for codependence, regardless of our gender.

Traditional Men's Roles and Unhealthy Helping and Giving

When you think about it, perhaps it's unsurprising there aren't large gender differences in unhealthy helping and giving. After all, both boys and girls may have the personality traits predisposing people to dysfunctional helping and giving. Men and women can be other-centered, empathic people that subordinate themselves to others and think it's their duty to take care of others. Boys, as well as girls, can be set up for codependent relationships by absent, difficult, abusive, or neglectful parents. And while there are aspects of traditional femininity that promote unhealthy helping, there are also aspects of traditional masculinity that promote men's excessive self-sacrifice for others.

One of these aspects is the male-as-family-provider role. This is the expectation that good men provide materially for their loved ones. Indeed, I've seen cases where fathers continued to behave consistently with this role well into their daughters' and sons' adulthood. In doing so, they acted consistently with their beliefs about what a good father does. The thought of reducing their giving to their adult children therefore created dissonance and kept them doing it. Their definition of loving father was so narrow that they didn't know how else to show their caring even if their giving hampered their children's maturity.

In some cultures like Taiwan, sons, especially first sons, have heavy family responsibilities. They're expected to obey their parents and demonstrate loyalty and obedience to parents and to put their family's needs before their own. Studies of codependency in Taiwanese college students find that men are higher in codependency than women. [80]

Many cultures teach that good men demonstrate their love (and masculinity) through the provision of money and material goods. Giving men sometimes attract relationship partners who expect them to subsidize their many material wants. Some takers reduce their male partners to success objects, valued to the extent they can satisfy the taker's material desires. They take advantage of giving men who have internalized their role as provider. For example, to keep his partner happy, Chris felt compelled to take his partner to expensive restaurants and clubs and on costly trips, even though he couldn't really afford it. This induced him to work overtime at a job he hated so he could keep up with his credit card bills and meet the needs of his adored but insatiable taker.

There's also a way in which many cultures hold up a heroic, chivalrous "man-as-protector" masculinity as a gold standard of masculinity. This archetype appears in many stories, toys, and media marketed to boys and men (movies and video games, especially). It's the knight in shining armor rescuing the damsel in distress (or the action hero that does), the solider whose brave actions fend off invaders and save the lives of his fellow citizens, and the man that rescues the town from the criminals that are terrorizing it. It's the heroic firefighter, cop, or soldier, the father protecting his family after the apocalypse or from the aliens. Rescuing can make you feel like you're being a good and honorable man, that is, if it's part of your masculinity script. While in some ways, this is a positive aspect of traditional masculinity, it gets some men into helping and giving trouble.

Qualifying the Role of Culture and Gender

It's tricky to make generalizations about the ways culture contributes to unhealthy helping and giving because culture is many things, and people vary in how strongly they identify with their culture's values and how they enact them. Personal values don't always correspond with cultural ones. [81] Social norms, such as the *social responsibility norm,* which suggests we have a duty to help those less fortunate, and the *reciprocity norm,* which prescribes we help those that have helped us, are also common worldwide, but clearly these norms and values are no guarantee of helping. Not only might other norms (like "mind your own business") contradict these, but some people accept these norms more than others. Indeed, you might remember from Chapter 4 that consistently helpful people tend to be more committed to values consistent with the social responsibility norm and experience more guilt if they don't help or share their resources. A person may have collectivist values even though their primary culture has individualist ones (or vice versa).

We also operate in multiple, unique, and overlapping cultures based on our gender, ethnicity, age, religion, class, nationality, etc., that may differ in values and in importance to our identity and how we define ourselves, and that vary in the norms that may promote unhealthy giving and taking. For example, many Americans are bicultural, simultaneously moving between individualistic and collectivistic American cultures. Some members of a religion are devout and are more influenced by the religion's culture (they internalize it more) and other members of the same religion not so much. Your friendship group's culture may prescribe sacrificing for group members while your family culture does not.

Gender also has varying effects on unhealthy helping and giving because of variation in gender roles and norms and how strongly these are enforced. What it means to be a man or woman, boy or girl, also varies based on other social categories such as our religion, ethnicity, age, and sexual orientation (this is the concept of *intersectionality*). And some families and communities strongly reward and model traditional gender roles and families, but other families and communities, not so much.

It's also difficult to make sweeping statements about gender because gender isn't as straight-forward as it appears at first glance. While it's common to think of gender as a binary where man/male and woman/female are clear-cut and the only possible identity categories, the truth is more complicated. Most of us have characteristics considered more typical of men, although we are women, and vice versa. Some people have a gender identity that's different from their birth-assigned gender (transgender people) and others are born with chromosomal and anatomical features of both males and females (intersex people). People also vary in how much their self-definition and behavior match what their culture defines as gender appropriate (how *gender-typed* they are). And people vary in *gender centrality* (the importance of gender relative to their other identities). Gender is complicated.

It's also risky to generalize about the influence of culture and gender because other factors, such as personality and personal history, play equally and sometimes more important roles in unhealthy helping and giving. Your personal beliefs about your moral obligation to help and how important being a helpful person is to your self-concept, may have a greater influence on your giving than cultural or gender norms. And because behavior is often a function of how person variables (like personality and experience) interact with situational variables (like social norms and roles), it's likely that personal factors interact with cultural messages prescribing giving to others, making unhealthy helping and giving more common in some people than others.

Self-reflection is required to determine the role that culture and gender play in our personal helping and giving patterns. If, however, you strongly identify as a member of a gender or culture that prescribes sacrificing for others, it may be worthwhile to consider whether you're being overly rigid in your enactment of helping and giving norms. You might also consider whether your actions really promote the welfare of the group and its members, or are really more about getting others to think that you're a good group citizen. You might also think about the long-term sustainability of your self-sacrifice and how you can better balance taking care of yourself while taking care of others.

So, gender and culture might be an important piece of a person's personal unhealthy helping and giving puzzle, or they might not. Box 8.1 helps you consider the influence of gender and culture on your helping and giving.

Box 8.1 How Does Your Culture and Gender Impact Your Helping and Giving?

1. How might the various cultures important to you affect your dysfunctional helping and giving? For example, does your religious culture support helping such that you experience dissonance (internal conflict) if you set helping or giving boundaries? Does your culture prescribe taking care of group members that can't take care of themselves?
2. To what extent were you raised to be a traditional woman or a traditional man? How does being a good woman or a good man as defined by you and your culture affect your over-giving, enabling, and rescuing? Does setting helping and giving boundaries create internal conflict by going against this vision of good woman or good man?
3. How could the withdrawal of your assistance be consistent with being a good woman or a good man or member of your culture? For example, does your culture also embrace the saying, "God helps those that help themselves"? Is promoting an adult child's dependence truly consistent with being a good mother or father?

Nine

Healthy Helping and Giving Boundary Setting

"You need to set some boundaries with her. You're not doing her or yourself any favors by continuing to bail her out," John said to his friend Terry for what seemed like the millionth time.

"I know, I know," Terry replied. "But you don't know her. She never met a boundary she didn't push and I never made one she couldn't push to the breaking point."

"I would just tell her you're done rescuing her and it's time for her to be more responsible. Case closed."

"Yeah, you probably would. But I'm not like you. I guess I'm just not that assertive. I try, but somehow she doesn't take me seriously and I always end up giving in. I'm just not good at saying 'no' and sticking to it."

"Well you better get good at it if you don't want to go through life being her doormat."

"Yeah, I know," Terry said, "Let's talk about something else."

Setting limits on our service to others is challenging for many reasons. Prior chapters suggest people have trouble setting good boundaries around their helping and giving because they:

- Feel guilty or anticipate feeling guilty if they don't help or give
- Fear other people's anger, emotion, abandonment, or rejection if they don't help or give
- Are able to satisfy unconscious emotional needs with their helping and giving
- Believe nice people should always put others before themselves
- Believe excessive helping and giving is required by their culture or by their gender or social role (parent, friend, daughter, son, sibling, etc.)
- Need to feel competent, like a hero, or like a generous person to boost self-esteem
- Want to atone for past sins
- Use their sacrifice and suffering to get and stay close to the recipients of their help and giving
- Are highly empathic, motivating them to act to relieve others' distress (and their own)
- Are rewarded by feeling competent or heroic, or by helper's high
- Haven't learned how to set good helping boundaries from important role models
- Have low self-esteem and don't think what they want or need is as important as what others want or need

These are all good explanations for why people have trouble setting healthy helping and giving boundaries. But some helping and giving problems are also assertiveness problems where people don't have the skills to assertively say no to helping requests or to end unhealthy or unwanted helping and giving arrangements. People may hear the tolling bells of unhealthy giving but lack confidence in their ability to peacefully set boundaries that won't harm the relationship or create drama. They lack self-efficacy in this regard so they aren't that motivated to try. This chapter includes many tips for the effective setting of healthy helping and giving boundaries. And as an added bonus, these techniques can eliminate or minimize potential drama and relationship damage.

Passivity In Unhealthy Helping and Giving Relationships

Many unhealthy givers exhibit passive, unassertive behavior in their relationships with others. They don't stand up for themselves and they comply with others' unreasonable requests. They don't feel they have the right to say no, or to put their needs above (or even equal to) other people's needs. Because setting appropriate giving boundaries is difficult for them, they're susceptible to unhealthy helping and giving relationships and to exploitation by difficult takers.

As described by psychologists Robert Alberti and Michael Emmons in a classic book on assertiveness, unassertive (passive) people deny themselves, allow others to choose for them, and feel inhibited, hurt, and anxious. [82] Likewise, passive givers stuff their reservations and keep giving, but meanwhile feel hurt and resentful they're the only ones giving, compromising, and bearing the costs of the relationship. Over time they feel diminished and abused in the relationship.

Due to fears of rejection or conflict and a desire to be nice, passive givers are prone to indirect verbal expressions of their boundaries. They drop hints about needing to pull back on their help or giving, or about their hopes that the taker will step up and take care of their own responsibilities. This passive approach is often ineffective and frustrating because these subtle messages frequently go unheard—the message sent by the giver isn't the one received by the taker.

Bobbi typified this by what she said to her son Jack. "Maybe you could think about looking for a job," she said, when what she really meant was, "It's time for you to get a job. It's too much for me to support you and you're at the age where it's time to support yourself." And, because of her fear of upsetting Jack, she said it in such a gentle, questioning tone that her strong feelings about the matter were further obscured. Jack took this understated message literally and thought his mother was only asking that he *think* about looking for a job.

So, when a giver talks about their declining finances, heavy workload, or ill health while hoping a taker will take the hint, most of the time they're wasting their breath. When it comes to reading between the lines of a subtle verbal message, some takers simply can't (their decoding skills aren't that great) and some takers simply won't (due to their personality traits or addictions).

Unhealthy givers also passively communicate their desire for change indirectly through non-verbal communications. But once again, these clues to their feelings may go unheard. Others may not notice or interpret their sighs, hesitations, grumbling, frowny-face, or reduced perkiness in their presence, as evidence of their dissatisfaction with the helping or giving arrangement. Some are really clueless and indirect doesn't work with them (they're just not that sensitive to other people's subtle cues). And although a giver may think their feelings about the matter are written all over their face, a taker may not know how to "read face" (some people have trouble decoding nonverbal communication).

Then of course are those takers that deliberately feign ignorance of passive, indirect messaging. These people know darn well what the giver is saying but ignore the giver's passive signaling so they can continue to receive the giver's bounty.

Passive messages also feel manipulative to some people who rebel by pretending they didn't receive them. They don't get that the giver's intent is to set boundaries quietly and without fuss. They experience passive, polite messages as passive-aggressive. These people will pretend they're unaware of your displeasure as long as you express it passively.

In pronounced cases of giver passivity, the giver hides their feelings so well the recipient hasn't a clue the giver feels unappreciated, burdened, and hurt. So the recipient continues to take while unbeknownst to them, the giver is increasingly dissatisfied with the situation.

This is kind of is silly when you think about it. People don't know how you feel unless you express your feelings. For example, a woman wrote to an advice columnist. The problem: she agreed to let her friend bring a few of her friends to her dinner party. Now every time she has an event, her friend invites her friends to come along. The columnist suggested the friend "had a lot of nerve and no manners." While this may very well be true, it's also true that the hostess gave more than she wanted because of her unassertiveness. And her friend didn't know it was a problem because she let it go on for so long. Like many passive givers she expected others to read her mind. She then held it against the non-psychic other for being inconsiderate. Not only is this a bit silly, it's a bit unfair. If you never tell people (in a way they can hear it) that you're not okay with the helping or giving situation, is it fair to hold it against them? After all, just how are they supposed to know? Unfortunately, the burden is often on us to be more honest and direct about our helping or giving boundaries. Sometimes we need be more assertive even if it's outside our comfort zone.

Passive-Aggressiveness in Unhealthy Helping and Giving Relationships

When givers are reluctant to speak up, they often become increasingly hurt, angry, and resentful. As they try to mask their anger and get others to change, they become *passive-aggressive.* Passive aggressive behavior occurs when we indirectly express our anger, hurt, or resentment. Passive-aggressive communications aren't blatantly angry, aggressive, or mean, but they have an undercurrent of anger, contempt, or resentment. Takers are often confused by these dual, contradictory messages they hear from their giver.

Passive-aggressive behavior usually occurs because we want to be a selfless giving person and so we stifle our dissatisfaction. When we're conflict-avoidant yet lack confidence in our ability to assert ourselves nicely, passive-aggressive communication feels safer than being direct. Unfortunately, our anger and resentment end up "leaking" into our comments and behavior. Of course, some people deliberately act passive-aggressively hoping it will take the place of the more direct, assertive behavior they're uncomfortable with. And, if their message is not well-received, they can more easily deny its meaning.

Verbal forms of passive aggressiveness include sarcastic comments or jokes ("It'll probably be just me and Robert, growing old together," a mother said to her friend in front of Robert, her adult son who lived with her). Backhanded compliments that communicate the giver's dissatisfaction by packaging it with a positive are also experienced by takers as passive-aggressive ("You're really good with computers. You know, you could use that to get a good job instead of just playing video games"). Passive-aggressive behavior may also be nonverbal, such as the "silent treatment" or "cold shoulder." Some givers communicate their unhappiness with subtle rejection of the taker, for example, refusing to engage in friendly chit-chat, and offering curt responses to direct questions.

Other examples of passive-aggressive behaviors include using snarky notes or texts to make requests or complaints. For example, Sarah was angry she was still supporting her friend Bethany, who moved in with her five months ago. Bethany broke her many promises to get a job and contribute financially. But Sarah was also conflicted because she wanted to be a good friend. From work Sarah texted Bethany, "Since you don't have a job and aren't doing anything, I'd appreciate it if you would wash your dirty dishes and take care of that pile of mildewing towels you left in the bathroom. I'm working so I don't have time."

Sometimes passive-aggressive givers give double-edged gifts ("Here's my old computer. Maybe you can use it to find a job."), or they will make the other wait for their assistance to show their displeasure. These are all indirect ways of expressing anger and resentment. If called on it, they may deny it ("I'm not mad at you, I'm just tired"; "That's not what I meant at all, you misunderstood"; or, "You're being too sensitive, I was just joking").

Like passive behavior, passive-aggressive behavior is largely ineffective but because of its aggressive edge, it carries a higher risk of relationship conflict. Some takers are angered or irritated by these indirect messages because they feel the giver is deliberately mean and critical, but cowardly. Some get mad because these messages are confusing and mixed ("What are they trying to say to me and which part of the message should I listen to—the part that says they don't mind giving or the part that really seems to mind giving?"). This leads them to respond to the aggressive piece of the message with a bit of aggression of their own (such as disrespect to the giver), making conflict spiraling likely.

Unhealthy givers aren't always the only ones acting passive-aggressively. In fact, many takers are masters of passive-aggressiveness. For example, when givers put terms and conditions on their giving or demand that takers stick to helping agreements, some takers get mad. They express their anger by stalling. They pretend to forget or that they didn't hear requests. They feign incompetence or comply with task requests but do a poor job. They make under-their-breath sarcastic comments in response to a request, deliberately violate agreed-upon rules or agreements, and are ungrateful.

Few givers are entirely passive or passive-aggressive in their interactions with takers. Most are at least occasionally assertive (let's build on that!) and some periodically get angry and aggressive (let's do less of that!). But unhealthy helping and giving relationships often involve some degree of passivity. After all, the giver consistently puts others' interests ahead of their own, and doesn't set healthy boundaries around their helping or giving.

Aggressiveness in Unhealthy Helping and Giving Relationships

Aggressive people forcefully advocate for their own interests, sometimes shouting, manipulating, shaming, blaming, or bullying others to get their way. Alberti and Emmons point out that aggressive people often lead others to feel hurt, defensive, and humiliated. Difficult takers often rely on aggression to get us to help or give, or keep us helping and giving. But even typically passive givers may become aggressive after a long martyr-like period of enabling, giving, or rescuing others. They get angry and go for broke, angrily setting their boundaries and shaming the taker. They say things like:

- "Your irresponsible behavior leaves me no choice but to say you can't use my car! Don't ever ask to borrow anything of mine ever again!"
- "It's your own fault you're in this predicament so no, I won't bail you out! If you'd done what I suggested to begin with we wouldn't be having this conversation!"
- "I'm sick and tired of having to rescue you because you never take responsibility for yourself! You're a big fat adult baby! Well, I'm done taking care of your sorry baby ass!
- "You disgust me and I refuse to enable your addiction any more! If you want to kill yourself that's your business but I will no longer be a party to it!"
- "You need to stop acting like you're royalty and take care of yourself like everyone else! I don't know where you got the idea you're better than everyone else but I'm done!"

But these statements aren't assertive, they're blatantly aggressive. Although the giver may very well have something to be angry about, aggressive boundary setting usually backfires.

Although assertiveness is about standing up for yourself, always remember it's not about setting your boundaries disrespectfully and with anger; that's being aggressive (people often confuse the two so this bears repeating). Aggressively set boundaries are occasionally necessary but they usually come with relationship costs. While sometimes that's okay, if preservation of a relationship is important, then setting your boundary in anger is a bad choice. Angrily set boundaries usually trigger a chain reaction of nastiness and hurt that can erode and even destroy a relationship. This is just a natural dynamic of human conflict. When you're angry, you don't choose your words carefully and you're more likely to set your boundary in a highly critical way leading to the taker's defensiveness and counterattack. That fuels your anger and leads to more angry defensive exchanges (conflict spiralling!). Then, once you calm down a little, the tendency is to feel guilty for being such a jerk, and that sometimes leads to backing away from a needed boundary.

Assertiveness in Unhealthy Helping and Giving Relationships

If passive behavior is too soft and aggressive behavior is too hard, then assertive behavior is just right. It's neither passive nor aggressive and it's a skill almost anyone can develop. As Alberti and Emmons say, assertive behavior is self-expressive, honest, direct and firm, and respectful of the rights of others. Like I say when teaching about assertiveness, assertive behavior involves being simple and direct, truthful yet tactful about your boundary, and tailoring your message to the recipient. Here are some examples of assertive statements that communicate helping and giving boundaries:

- "I can see you're in a bind, and although I sympathize, I can't help you. You'll be okay, I have faith in you, you'll figure it out."
- "I know you need this job and you're trying to stop drinking but I have to let you go. I've tried to help by giving you loads of chances but

things haven't changed. I wish you well but I've come to the realization that your employment here isn't working out."

- "Remember how the last time I lent you money, I said not to ask again because I would say "no"? I really meant it. I'm so sorry you're in a tight situation again because I do care about you, but that really was the last time for me."
- "I know that I've done ____ for you in the past, but I'm no longer willing to do that. I'm sorry if it comes as a surprise, but I've reached the conclusion it's too big a strain on me."
- "As of [date], I will no longer do _____for you. I know I'm changing the rules since I've always been willing to do this for you in the past, but it's time for you to take care of yourself. I'm convinced it would be wrong of me to continue to hold you back from independence."
- "As much as I love you, I'm no longer willing to do this for you. It's too much for me, and it's preventing you from doing what you need to do to get better. I will however be happy to drive you to your medical or therapist appointments."
- "I appreciate that you think I have the ability to help solve this problem but I am overbooked and I absolutely have to decline."
- "Thank you so much for acknowledging what I did to make our past events so successful. I'm complimented you'd ask me to help again but unfortunately I have too much going on and I just can't be involved this year."
- "I'd love to host the event again but I hope you'll understand that I don't have the energy I used to. So, the only way that I can do it is if everyone brings something and helps clean up afterward."

I want to point out something very important about the above assertive statements: When an explanation is offered for declining or withdrawing help, notice that it's brief and somewhat vague, and all on you. While it may be true we're withdrawing our assistance or saying no because they've failed to live up to agreements or because they're making bad choices or being irresponsible or have taken advantage, that's kind of beside the point. The real point is to set clear boundaries simply and without drama, not make them admit it's their fault we need to set boundaries. Offering specific reasons, especially ones having to do with them, usually leads to defensiveness and argumentativeness. If you're not good at arguing and they are, that can lead you to back away from your boundaries. A discussion might also kick up your guilt and make you retreat from your boundaries.

It's also important to remember that *we have the right to say no* so their acceptance of our boundary isn't really necessary. Sometimes givers forget it's their time, money, effort, etc. and it's therefore their right to decide what to do with these personal resources. They want the taker to understand and accept their decision so they don't feel so mean, or to get the taker to accept responsibility for the boundary. They spend far too much time justifying themselves to the taker, which opens the door for the taker's defensiveness and argument. Sometimes that's the slippery slope to a weakening of a needed boundary. Like I said, it's generally best just to keep it simple and to the point.

So, if they try to argue or discuss, don't even go there. Instead, calmly and *with no judgment in your tone*, say something along the lines of:

- "I know this is hard for you to hear, but my mind is made up."
- "I'm glad I was able to give so much for so long but things have changed and I must stop now. I trust you'll figure something out and manage without me."
- "All I have to say is that I love you but I'm sure in my decision. It's up to me to decide how to use my resources and this is something I no longer want to do."
- "I know this is scary for you, and I wish you only the best, but I'm sure this is what I need to do."
- "I'm sorry if my decision makes things harder for you. Although I'm no longer willing to give to you in this way, I hope you can respect my decision and we can stay friends."
- "I know I've always done this in the past and that everyone's used to it, but I can't do it anymore. Trust me, we'll all adjust before long. Everyone will be all right."

Then calmly remove yourself from the situation or change the subject.

Even if your taker doesn't try to argue, they may test you to see if you mean it. They may drag their feet, escalate their neediness, or even concoct an emergency. Or, they may just continue to ask. This means you should prepare to repeat your assertive statement multiple times, especially if in the past you've made similar statements only to cave in later. If you haven't stuck to your boundaries in the past, they know that although you say no sometimes, there also are times when you give in (remember from Chapter 6 that partially reinforced behaviors are resistant to extinction). Keep in mind that it may take a while before they take your boundary seriously. Be prepared to restate your limit, gently terminate the conversation, and repeat as necessary.

Above all, be somewhat matter-of-fact rather than all dramatic and emotional about it. Stay as calm and emotionally even as you can. As psychologist Harriet Lerner points out in her book *The Dance of Intimacy* (1989), anger is likely to be met with anger, intensity only breeds more intensity, anxiety only more anxiety, etc. [83] And remember, no blaming or shaming leading to defensiveness and fight, just be simple and direct about what you will or won't do.

It's Not Just What's Said But How It's Said

Assertive behavior is partly about what you say (the simple and straight-forward words or verbal communication) but it's also about *how* you say it. Your tone, facial expressions, and how you position your body while you say it (your nonverbal communication) are all part of assertive communication. For instance, your tone matters a lot. Go back to the last bulleted list of assertive statements and say them with different tones of voice and you'll see what I mean. Some of them can sound passive-aggressive, aggressive, or assertive, depending on *how* they are said.

When asserting your boundaries try to use a confident, well-modulated, pleasant, matter-of-fact tone. On the one hand, if you mumble, speak too softly, sound whiny, or hesitate too much, you'll sound too passive and your boundary may not be taken seriously. Don't sound like you're asking for their permission or for their blessing of your boundary. On the other hand, if you speak too loudly, forcefully, or harshly, your message may be perceived as aggressive and will lead to an aggressive response from the other. Assertive messages are communicated with a smooth, calm, confident, non-hesitant flow of speech.

If you're face-to-face (which is ideal), strengthen your assertive message with occasional eye contact, but don't insist on sustained, locked eye contact because people tend to experience this as aggressive. Don't look down the whole time like you're embarrassed or unsure about your boundary, but don't stare them down. Have good posture (avoid a slumped, passive posture that communicates uncertainty). Orient your body towards, rather than away from them.

Finally, you should understand that both culture and individual differences may affect how your intended assertiveness is interpreted and you should match your message to the recipient as best as you can. Use what you know about the other person to adjust your message. For example, you wouldn't want to make direct eye contact if that's considered disrespectful in the other's culture, or cast your eyes downward if that's considered disrespectful.

Take individual differences into account when you craft your message. You probably know some people are kind of dense and won't hear your assertive message unless it is stated more strongly; you practically have to hit them over the head with it or at least repeat it a few times before they get it (especially if you've been passive or inconsistent with boundaries in the past). With these people you may have to kick it up a notch and try again. Conversely, other people interpret that same strong message as aggressive, rather than assertive. If the other acts hurt and defensive and counter-attacks, these are indicators your message was experienced as shaming and blaming. Apologize for your harshness and kick it down a notch and try again. Once again, remember: no blaming or shaming just be simple and direct about what you will or won't do.

Assertiveness With Immature or Addicted Others

Immature and addicted takers present the greatest challenges to our assertiveness. They may try to change our minds by crying, arguing, threatening self-harm, complimenting, pleading incompetence or helplessness, or refusing to take no for an answer. Some will bully you to get what they want. If a taker is aggressive, attempts at boundary setting can quickly turn nasty when you decline a rescuing opportunity or attempt to terminate an unhealthy helping or giving arrangement. When faced with our boundaries, some takers push our guilt buttons so hard we feel bruised afterwards. These takers wear down our resolve and can weasel us into retreating from needed boundaries.

Difficult takers often respond to boundary setting as if it's aggressive and victimizes them. As a result, they're especially prone to defensive responses and manipulation. They may attack the giver, calling them selfish or heartless, and they may accuse the giver of not caring for them. Feeling entitled to our resources or care, they may get angry when we deny them what they believe is theirs. In these situations it's important not to take the bait by getting angry and defensive and counter-attacking, for example, by attacking them for their irresponsibility. This will get you off-track and aggravate the situation. If there's ever a time to turn the other cheek, this is it.

Immature and addicted takers are also among the most persistent of takers, ignoring and testing your boundaries to see if you mean it. Instead of reacting with anger or irritation, or caving in to their demands, say something like, "I know you're not happy about this, but I've made up my mind and I'm confident you can handle it." Repeat as necessary and eventually they'll catch on.

As they say in sports, sometimes the best defense is a good offense. It pays to admit when our taker is of the immature or manipulative variety. That way, we're prepared to restate our boundary while refusing to participate in unproductive dialogue. Likewise, it pays to acknowledge if a taker is violence-prone and might respond to your boundaries with aggression. Domestic violence organizations and hotlines can provide advice (in the US, call 1-800-799-SAFE).

Developing Your Here-and-Now Boundary Setting Skills

Here-and-now boundary setting occurs when you immediately set limits when presented with a helping or giving "opportunity." For example, when someone asks you for money, a favor, your drugs, your time, your car, to cover for them, to pay the costs of their irresponsibility, bend the rules for them, etc. you have the opportunity in that very moment to assertively set a limit on your giving.

Here-and-now boundary setting is a relatively simple matter of assertively declining to help or give. It's elegant in its simplicity. You just gracefully, simply, but assertively say "no" when asked. Something like, "I'm sorry, I can't, I have other stuff to do," or "Sorry, I'm not comfortable doing that but I know things will work out for you," usually does the trick.

You also must be assertive with yourself when presented with another's dilemma. You have to override your reflexive tendency to help or give by monitoring yourself (switch to System 2!). For instance, while you once automatically responded to your feelings of empathy by offering help or by saying yes to a request for help, now you practice pausing so you can think before you act. If there are red flags warning of trouble, or you realistically cannot spare the resources to give (whether it's time, money, or energy), you must stop yourself from intervening. Use assertive self-talk, for example:

- "I know better than to do this so I won't."
- "I better not intervene because I will be sorry if I do."
- "I don't need to do anything to help other than to listen."
- "I can say 'no' and everyone will be fine."
- "I wish I could, but I know from experience I really can't.
- "I'm not going to give more than I can afford to, I always regret it later."
- "I need to say no even if they might be unhappy with me.
- "This is not my circus, and not my monkeys; this is not my problem to solve."

When faced with another's difficulty, instead of jumping in to rescue, you can just nod sympathetically, and say vague, soothing things like:

- "Wow, that's a challenging situation! Fortunately, you're up to the challenge. You're a survivor."
- "That's so stressful but after all you've been through, I know you'll figure it out and get through it."

- "What a tough situation! Have you started thinking about a plan?"

You can provide support without going overboard. Many givers are surprised to find that emotional support is all many people seek when they complain about their misfortune or poverty. Not every complainer is looking for your rescue. Sometimes listening is all that's needed from you. And some people ask just in case you might say yes. They're really okay with you saying no but thought it was worth asking.

Assertively and respectfully saying no to other people's requests or hints for assistance often takes practice. You can do this in front of a mirror or through experience, but role-playing (as ridiculous as that sounds), is really one of the best ways to get better at assertiveness. This type of role-playing involves no costumed sex (sorry!). Instead, a friend, loved one, or therapist plays the role of the taker while you play yourself assertively setting your boundary. When you practice with another person, you can get needed feedback on the words you choose, the tone you use, and whether your body communicates confidence or uncertainty. Box 9.1 provides a role-playing exercise to help you perfect your here-and-now assertiveness skills.

Box 9.1 Perfecting Your Here-and-Now Assertiveness Skills with Role-Playing

This activity is intended to help you refine your assertive behavior and it requires a partner (a therapist is ideal but a friend can work). Make sure that your partner understands the difference between passive, assertive, and aggressive behavior and pays attention to your tone and body language as well as the words you choose.

You play the person that's assertively setting the boundary and your partner plays the taker. Both of you should try to do this *as realistically as possible.*

Instruct your partner to behave as they think the "character" in the role-play would act.

After each role-play, ask for feedback on whether the boundary-setting was assertive, aggressive, or passive and ask your partner to comment on your tone, eye contact, and body language. Talk with your partner about how your assertive communication can be improved.

1. Your friend once again asks to borrow $50 for her utility bill because she gave money to her son so he could pay his bills.
2. Your co-worker asks you to work his shift (again) because "something came up."
3. Your son asks to borrow your car (again) because he doesn't have time before work to gas up his own car.
4. Your addicted adult child who has a suspended license demands that you drive them to meet a drug connection.
5. Your procrastinating co-worker complains to you that she doesn't know how she's going to meet her deadline. Meanwhile, you didn't procrastinate and you've completed your share of the work. You think she's hinting for a rescue because in the past, when she's done this, you've bailed her out.
6. Your relative, who has a gambling problem, calls and asks you for money even though they already owe you $2000.
7. Your friend wants you to tell their romantic partner that they were at your house last night when they were off romancing someone they met at a bar. Although you've covered for them before, you're not comfortable enabling their infidelity and don't want to do it again.
8. Once again, your neighbors want you to take care of their pets while they go out of town for the weekend. You didn't mind doing it a few times a year but now you're doing it at least once a month. The pet-sitting cuts into your weekend activities since you have to go to their house at least three times a day. You're starting to resent it and want to say no the next time they ask.

9. You're asked to rescue an ineffective committee by assuming the leadership position ("We need you, no one else can do it as well as you!") but you need to say "no" to avoid being overloaded.
10. Choose a situation from your life in which you needed to assertively set here-and-now boundaries but had trouble doing so, or a choose an anticipated request for your help or giving. Explain it to your partner and role-play.

Developing Your Planned Boundary Setting Skills

Sometimes you'll need to use *planned boundary setting* to let someone know that you're ending a helping or giving arrangement you have with them. This is just what it sounds like—you plan a boundary-setting talk ahead of time, choosing an appropriate time and place and planning what you're going to say before meeting. You may need planned boundary setting when you want to terminate an ongoing unhealthy helping or giving arrangement. For example, you've been paying someone's rent, driving them to work, letting them live with you, or giving them expensive gifts, and you need to stop, or want to stop. With planned boundary setting you set a boundary *before* you're expected to help or give again.

Planned boundary setting is called for when you don't want to pull the rug out from under someone you've been helping or giving to because it seems too rude or unfair. When you'd rather courteously give them some time to make other arrangements, transition to independence, or get used to the idea of your lessened giving, planned boundary setting is called for. For example, you might plan to tell your neighbor you won't be giving him a ride to and from work anymore, your 24-year-old she needs to move out, or your adult children that you're cutting back on monetary birthday or holiday gifts.

Preparation and courage are required for planned boundary setting. You carefully prepare what you want to say and practice it ahead of time. This is no small thing since careful word choice and presentation can minimize the likelihood of defensiveness and conflict escalation. Another advantage is you go into the boundary-setting situation prepared to stay calm and rational despite any drama from the taker. You've got your words ready and you're set to deflect any nonsense and stick to the point. For example, many "interventions" with addicted people are examples of planned boundary setting where loved ones read letters to the person expressing their concerns and boundaries. Prior to the intervention they meet and plan the event.

Here are the basic steps of planned boundary setting: [84]

1. Think about the best time and place. Timing and location can matter as far as your safety and their receptiveness.
2. Start by saying how much you love/like/appreciate them (something true and nice but short). For example, you might tell the neighbor that you really like having them as a neighbor or your 24-year-old that you love her and value your relationship with her.
3. State the boundary simply and assertively, without triggering defensiveness. Avoid shaming them or blaming them. Keep it focused on what you will or will not do. If they start to get worked up, stay calm and gently reassure them by saying something like, "I'm sorry this is hard for you but you'll be okay."
4. Take responsibility for your part in the fractured giving relationship to reduce their defensiveness and increase acceptance of your boundary. For example, you may be responsible for concealing your dissatisfaction, or for continuing the arrangement despite your dwindling resources. You can say things like:
   - "Look, this is on me. You couldn't have known this was a problem for me since I didn't tell you and I kept on doing it."
   - "I'm sorry if my actions led you to believe that I could do this indefinitely."
   - "I should've been clear I intended that to be a short-term thing."
   - "I want to apologize for acting distant and grumpy towards you. I should have been more direct about my need to change our arrangement."

You may also bear some responsibility for promoting their dependence to satisfy your own emotional needs. If this is true, it helps to take that responsibility. For example, one person said, "Truth is, I've been afraid of being alone and I've made it easy for you to stay. I wanted to keep you close to me where I could make sure you were all right. But now I've thought about it, I'm know I'm holding you back. I don't want to do that to you because I care about you."

5. Keep word count low. Although you'll say a bit more than you would if you were engaging in here-and-now boundary setting, you should still keep it to the point while sounding confident and matter-of-fact about your boundary.

   Here's an example of what one dad said to his 25 year-old son:

> Thanks for having lunch with me. You know you're one of the most important people in my life.
>
> But I have to tell you son, I need to change some things. You see, it's time for me to stop providing for you. In trying to take care of you, I've kept you from leading the independent life you should be living at this point in your life and I have to think about my retirement.
>
> So here's what's happening: when it's time to re-new my car insurance in two months, and my cellphone plan in three months, you'll have to get your own. Also, I feel that it's time for you to move out—it's time for you to go live your life and make your own way, and let's face it, we're not exactly getting along! You can stay with me for three more months so you can work more hours and figure out how to live on your income.
>
> I know this is a big change but every person has to make this transition and I have faith in you. I'm not abandoning

> you. You're always welcome to visit and although I want you to support yourself financially, I'm always here as an advisor and for moral support if you need me.

Although it may feel a little strange to plan your boundary-setting, as psychologist Harriet Lerner points out, planning and tact are what make truth-telling (and truth-hearing) possible in difficult situations. [85] Box 9.2 leads you through an exercise to help you design your planned boundary setting.

Box 9.2 Practice Planned Boundary Setting

Directions: Write down the answers to the following prompts. Ideally practice and obtain feedback before carrying out your planned boundary-setting effort. You may find it helpful to refer back to the chapter for examples.

1. Define your boundaries in a clear and specific way, including relevant details such as when it begins, what you will or will not do, and what they're expected to do.
2. What is the safest place, and the best day and time of day to talk to them?
3. Choose and write out what you're going to say to begin, ideally saying something truthful about the value of the relationship to you.
4. Following the assertiveness guidelines, write out what you can say to set your boundary with this person. To reduce defensiveness, write a couple of drafts until there's little in there that might shame or blame the other (see the discussion on assertiveness). Use your experience with them to inform your word choices.
5. Write out what you'll do if they get defensive, try to argue, or try to persuade you to back off your boundary. Think about how they act when they get defensive and how can you deflect it.
6. Write out what you might say to end the discussion.

7. Practice. You can do this in front of a mirror, with a video camera, or with a friend, loved one, or therapist. Pay attention to your tone, voice volume, eye contact and body language.

Note: Only set boundaries you're committed to keeping. Otherwise, you partially reinforce the behavior (see Chapter 6).

Dealing With Ambivalence Following Assertiveness

As they walk away (or terminate a phone conversation) after setting a boundary, givers may experience ambivalence. For example, I've been known to say, "Oh my God, am I a selfish or mean person? Will they be okay? I hope they're not mad at me!"

I call this *boundary guilt* and it's particularly common when we set boundaries and watch others bear their own consequences and struggle to take care of themselves. We can reduce this ambivalence by reminding ourselves that we're doing the right thing. For example, self-statements like these help me to reduce my ambivalence so I feel good about my boundary and stick to it:

- "It's their right to be displeased with my boundary but it's my right to set limits around what I will and won't do. After all, it's my money, time, effort, etc."
- "Their anger or displeasure is unfortunate and I wish they didn't feel that way, but I can handle it, and they will probably get over it."
- "I didn't make this decision lightly and it's the right thing for me to do even if they don't like me right now. I already know that the status quo can't continue."
- "I'm not a bad or mean person for setting this boundary. It's best for them, our relationship, and me. So, even if they can't see it right now, I know I'm doing the right thing."

- "I can't make them happy about my decision but that's okay. I wish they would understand my decision, but even if they don't, that's okay. Ultimately it's up to me what I will do for them and I know I can't give like that any more."
- "Although they're displeased with me right now, I have to do this because it makes it more likely they'll get the help they need, work their program, become independent, etc. My help isn't all that helpful in the long run. Withdrawing it gives them a chance to get better."
- "I hope they'll get it together and manage just fine without my help but if they don't, it's their choice, not my fault because I know they can do it if they choose to."
- "They'll be okay. They need to figure out how to make it on their own, without my constant intervention."

Some people find it helpful to write their affirmations on a piece of paper so they can refer to it to strengthen their resolve. It's also helpful to immediately obtain reinforcement from someone supportive of our boundary setting.

Chapter 10 provides additional guidance for managing the ambivalence that often accompanies (and sometimes hinders) our personal change.

Ten

Conclusion

If unhealthy helping and giving were a crime, I'd have a long rap sheet. I'd be skating on the thin ice of a judge's warning that if I violate parole one more time, I'm going to jail for good. But I think I'm finally rehabilitated. Thinking about my own unhealthy helping and giving through the lenses of psychology helped me understand why this is a problem for me, and what to do about it. It's also given me the confidence and strength I need to set appropriate boundaries when my helping or giving is in danger of crossing the line from healthy to unhealthy. I better understand why my helpful efforts didn't always produce the results I expected, and why they sometimes led others to resent me. I'm better at checking myself and my motives so that when I help, it's actually helpful and for the right reasons. This is my hope for you as well. But before I send you off into the world armed with the knowledge and skills to change your unhealthy helping and giving, read this chapter for a little extra guidance before moving forward.

Summing It Up: Take Away Messages

Let's begin with a brief summary of some of the main "take away messages" from this book.

Take Away Message 1: There's a Big Difference Between Healthy and Unhealthy Helping and Giving. Helping and giving aren't by definition good. Some types of helping and giving create unhealthy dependencies and reduce others' self-confidence, competencies, and life skills. Our help can prevent people from seeking treatment for addictions or psychiatric disorders, or from taking care of their mental or physical health. It can reduce both our ability to take care of ourselves and others' ability to take care of themselves. Helping and giving can also unexpectedly harm our relationships and our groups, and lead to our anger, resentment, and burnout. Acknowledging the harms of your helping may be important to reduce ambivalence and motivate your change. (See Chapters 1, 2, and 3)

Take Away Message 2: Taming Our Empathy (and Agreeableness) Promotes Healthy Helping and Giving. Your empathic response to other people's difficulties and suffering can motivate healthy helping and giving. But your empathy can also get you into big trouble when it leads you to respond and contribute to others' manufactured needs, and when it leads to impulsive rescues or giving you can't afford or sustain. You may have to sit with your alarm about others' dilemmas long enough to make a rational decision about whether you should honor your impulse to help (switch to Cognitive System 2). In other words, beware of the emotional reasoning mindtrap; your feelings in that moment may tell you must rescue or give but it might not be the best thing to do. And remember, others aren't always looking for your rescue when they tell you their troubles; sometimes they just need emotional support. (See Chapters 4, 7, and 9)

Take Away Message 3: Healthy Helping and Giving Sometimes Require Toning Down Our Conformity *to Prosocial Norms and Roles.* Sometimes our unhealthy helping and giving results from over-enacting gender or cultural norms calling for service to other people. We can twist and twirl prosocial helping norms that are normally good into excessive self-sacrifice and enabling that ultimately harm the group and its members. We need to discriminate between the positive prosocial helping these norms and roles are intended to promote, and the unhealthy helping or giving we're engaged in. We can be good women and men or members of our religion, culture or group without unhealthy helping and giving. (See Chapter 8)

Take Away Message 4: Addressing Emotional Issues Is Sometimes Necessary For Healthy Helping and Giving. Our helping and giving isn't always as generous and other-serving as we want to believe. It's often motivated by a desire to feel good about ourselves, to atone for past sins, and to get and stay close to others. Sometimes it arises from unresolved emotional issues rooted in childhood, or unhealthy early attachments. Healthy helping and giving sometimes require processing the issues from our past that led to our helping and giving troubles. (See Chapters 4, 5, 7, and 8)

Take Away Message 5: Unhealthy Helping and Giving Are Sometimes Family Traditions In Need of Change. Unhealthy helping and giving often have roots in our family of origin. We can mindlessly enact unhealthy helping and giving "scripts" learned from our parents. Unhealthy helping and giving may be family norms that prescribe enabling and rescuing lower-functioning family members. It pays to examine these family roots and their consequences and to consciously break from harmful family patterns (especially so we don't pass our unhealthy helping and giving habits on to our children). Family traditions are great but we should willingly let go of ones that ultimately harm the family unit and its members. (See Chapters 2, 5, and 6)

Take Away Message 6: Straightening Out "Crooked Thinking" Can Reduce Unhealthy Helping and Giving. One message in this book is that our own irrational thinking often causes and maintains our unhealthy helping and giving. For example, many givers are afraid that setting helping and giving boundaries makes them selfish (when it doesn't) or that others will be extremely mad at them and they won't be able to stand it (when they can, *if* it happens). They may falsely believe that people won't like them if they don't excessively self-sacrifice and that setting boundaries will lead to abandonment. But we can take charge of our heads and make better decisions about who and when to help. To do this, we can identify our irrational helping and giving beliefs, and then dispute and challenge them. (See Chapter 8)

Take Away Message 7: We Can Empower Ourselves to Become Healthy Helpers and Givers. Even if we feel entrapped in an unhealthy helping and giving relationship we can usually escape. (However, if a taker uses threats of violence to keep you giving, consult a domestic violence center or hotline like 1-800-799-SAFE to help you plan for safe escape). Even if we identify as codependent we can pull back when we see the red flags warning of a difficult taker or unhealthy helping and giving. We can address unresolved emotional issues leading to unhealthy helping and giving and build our boundary setting skills. We can check our empathy so it doesn't lead to impulsive, unsustainable helping. We can straighten out our crooked thinking. We can choose equitable relationships and break unhealthy helping and giving habits. We can use calm, clear, consistent assertive statements to set effective boundaries with most takers. (See Chapters 4-9)

Take Away Message 8: Continue to Be A Giving Person; Just Don't Give To Habitual Takers. Throughout the book, you read about difficult takers who manipulate to get others to do their work and take care of them so that they can avoid taking responsibility for themselves. They push the boundaries of our helping and giving in ways most people would be ashamed to. Their need for our help and giving is never-ending because they refuse to do what they need to do to be healthy, self-sufficient, or independent. Their need for others' intervention is manufactured by their own choices. Unlike most people, they're satisfied with getting by on our hard work and kindness. Learning to recognize these takers quickly is one key to healthy giving. Our helpful, giving energies are best directed to people that will use them to move forward in their lives. So watch for people that only help when there's something in it for them. Make sure your help doesn't prevent others from being full, contributing members of the group or society. If your help doesn't inspire and promote others' productivity and just makes it easy for them to slack, you're not helping in the right way, or you're dealing with a taker.

The Transtheoretical Model: Change is a Process

It's no small thing to change. Most people sort of build towards change, first admitting there's a problem and then preparing and enacting a plan. And of course, people run into challenges along the way that tempt them to give up. The *transtheoretical model of change* (also known as the "stages of change model") reminds us that it's normal to gradually move towards change, and that change often happens in fits and starts. [86]

If you read this book because you're concerned about the unhealthy giving of a loved one or friend, it pays to keep this in mind. Although it's tempting to push them to change, if they're not ready it may only lead them to avoid you or dig in their heels, especially if they feel judged. To gently push them in the direction of change listen non-judgmentally and say things like, "This happens to lots of people. Have you thought about reading a book about this? Going to a support group? Talking to a mental health professional?"

If you read this book because you're seeking to understand a difficult helping or giving situation, or your past unhealthy helping and giving, at the very least, you're in the transtheoretical model's *contemplation stage*. In the contemplation stage people realize there's an issue and they start thinking about it. The seeds of change may have been planted a while ago (the model also has a *precontemplation stage*), but the contemplation stage is where they sprout and begin to grow. Answer the questions in Box 10.1 to promote your movement through the contemplation stage.

Box 10.1 Promote Your Contemplation Stage

1. What do you think about your helping behavior? What realizations have you come to? What are you doing that needs to change?
2. What kinds of problems have your helping created?

3. After reading this book, what best explains why you do it and what you should do about it?

The *preparation stage* follows the contemplation stage as a person moves from acknowledging and thinking about the problem to getting ready to do something about it. For example, you may already be in the preparation stage and chose this book to prepare a strategy for change.

During the preparation stage, you may formulate a plan for setting a needed boundary. You might use the material from Chapter 9 to decide what to say and how to say it. Or, you might call a domestic violence (intimate partner violence) hotline or the police for assistance on how to safely terminate a relationship with a mean or violent taker. [87]

If your taker has a physical, medical, cognitive, or psychiatric disability the preparation stage may involve some research so that you can discern the line between healthy and unhealthy helping in this situation with this individual. Learn as much as you can about their condition (including visiting expert websites, online or local support groups for loved ones, and consulting the other's treatment professionals if possible). Try to accurately determine what their personal limitations truly are, how other people manage well with the condition, and how you can empower them to manage their own condition and live a full life. For example, NAMI, the National Alliance for the Mentally Ill, is a good resource for families and friends of those with psychiatric illness.

Answer the questions in Box 10.2 to promote your movement through the preparation stage.

Box 10.2 Promote Your Preparation Stage

Instructions: Write down the answers to these questions.

1. Do a quick skim of the table of contents. Which chapters resonated with you the most? Which concepts?
2. Looking back at those chapters and concepts, what specifically are you going to do to change? What tools will you use? What are the specifics of your change plan?

After the contemplation and preparation stages, it's time for the *action stage* of change where you move forward with your plans for healthy helping and giving. For example, your action stage might involve putting into practice plans for:

1. Terminating new relationships that push your codependence buttons (use your experience and newfound knowledge to identify "red flags" that warn of trouble—get out quick when you see them).
2. Distancing from or ending existing codependent and other unhealthy helping and giving relationships or, when that's not possible (for example if it's a close family member), redefining the relationship by setting and sticking to boundaries (for example, by refusing to bail them out or declining to take care of their responsibilities).
3. Thinking before you rescue.
4. Cultivating healthy relationships with higher functioning people (relationships that aren't based on their dysfunction and your care/support).
5. Getting counseling to address emotional issues underlying your unhealthy helping and giving.

Because this book offers lots of practical advice to help you set better boundaries around your helping, it may be a useful tool during your action stage. If you're already using the techniques in the book, you're already in the action stage.

Finally you should know that there are often steps forward and steps backward in the action stage. Sometimes people make progress only to regress back to the precontemplation stage. They go back to old habits and try to stifle their discomfort only to find themselves once again contemplating change. So hang in there with your change efforts—it's a process and takes time.

You may find it easier to act consistently for change if you have *social support* (support from other people). For example, it's easier to stick to your change plan if friends and loved ones serve as your cheerleaders as you set boundaries and work through ambivalence (therapists can provide great support as well). You should identify your change supporters, share your commitment to change (and your change plans), and provide regular progress reports. This makes you more accountable and increases consistent boundary setting.

Some people get their social support from 12-step programs for codependency or support groups for the loved ones of addicted people (such as CoDA or Al-Anon). Based on the 12-step model of Alcoholics Anonymous, these participant-led groups work through the twelve steps as applied to codependency and enabling. Not only is it comforting to be with people who understand your situation, you can also receive encouragement, be exposed to role models of change, and be inspired by the successes of group members. These groups aren't a good fit for everyone but they're key to the recovery of some unhealthy helpers and givers. Box 10.3 helps you identify social supports for your action phase.

Box 10.3 Securing Social Support For Your Action Phase

Instructions: Write down the answers to these questions.

1. What friends or loved ones are particularly concerned about your unhealthy helping and giving?

2. Which ones would make good coaches or cheerleaders as you move towards a healthier relationship with helping and giving?
3. Is a support group a desirable option for you? If so, take 15 minutes right now to identify the groups in your area. Or, consider starting one of your own.
4. After identifying your best sources of social support, make a public commitment to your change plan. Tell your supporters what you're going to do and ask them if you can count on their support as you move towards change. Communicate with them regularly as you work through the change process.

Exploring and Managing Change-Retarding Ambivalence

One thing that keeps us stuck in the contemplation or preparation stage, or causes us to regress once in the action stage, is our ambivalence about change. *Motivational interviewing* (MI), a therapeutic change approach, suggests acknowledging, exploring, and managing ambivalence is an important piece of the personal change puzzle. [88]

Ambivalance often keeps people stuck in their unhealthy helping and giving. Although on the face of it change seems straightforward, thoughts of change frequently bring cognitive dissonance (internal conflict). Cutting off assistance or reducing giving is consistent with knowing it's problematic, but inconsistent with a desire to be generous and selfless. If a giver believes the other might be harmed or upset if aid is withdrawn, setting boundaries can create dissonance. Dissonance is also likely if a giver fears boundaries might harm or end an important relationship. Ambivalence can stunt progress in the action stage. While there are things counting in favor of change, there are also things counting against it.

The cognitive-behavioral techniques discussed in Chapter 7 are useful for managing change-retarding ambivalence since ambivalence sometimes arises from faulty thinking and mind traps. Identifying and challenging our extreme and sometimes irrational thoughts around our helping is often critical to our moving forward and setting needed boundaries. You have to build up the thoughts that support your boundary setting and tear down the thoughts that pose barriers to healthy helping and giving.

For example, you're not a bad person if you don't rescue someone from their irresponsibility or if you terminate an unhealthy helping arrangement, so you shouldn't let that be a source of ambivalence. In fact, it could be argued that boundary setting is often what a good person should do.

Likewise, the odds are your relationship with the recipients of your help or giving will weather any boundaries you set, so fears about losing your relationship are probably an unnecessary or exaggerated source of your ambivalence. Most people will still like you and want to have relationships with you even if you don't excessively give, and if they don't, you have greater freedom to pursue healthier, more equitable relationships. Remember that even if people get mad when you limit your assistance, you can survive it and it's better than paying such a high price just to avoid someone being displeased with you. Besides, as I said before, when you think about it, helping or givng to others is no guarantee they won't get mad at you or that they will treat you well.

Helping professionals (psychologists, social workers, counselors) that use motivational interviewing encourage you to think about the discrepancy between your present behavior and your broader goals so that you'll be motivated to change your behavior. You can use the motivational interviewing activity in Box 10.4 to help you reduce your ambivalence.

Box 10.4 Use Motivational Interviewing To Reduce Your Ambivalence

Instructions: Write down the answers to these questions.

1. How is my continued helping or giving making it hard for me to accomplish important personal or family goals? (Such goals may be financial, professional, social, or related to your mental or physical health.)

2. How is my helping or giving actually unhelpful? How does it interfere with other person's long-term health, well-being, and autonomy rather than truly being helpful?

Look at your answers regularly when you feel ambivalent about setting boundaries around your helping and giving.

Working with a Trained Mental Health Professional

Throughout the book, I've suggested working with a therapist. For example, if an unstable self-esteem or guilt is a primary motivator for your unhealthy helping or giving, a therapist may be able to help.

A therapist may also be useful for working the material in this book. Doing the activities and talking over the results with a trained mental health professional can be almost magical if you identify a therapist that's a good match for you and you really want to change. [89] Working with a mental health professional on your helping and giving issues can keep you focused and accountable so that your change goals don't fall by the wayside.

In the United States, you'll probably have the most success with a licensed psychologist, social worker (often called an LCSW, or licensed clinical social worker), marriage and family therapist (often called an MFT), or professional counselor (often called an LPC, or licensed professional counselor). I don't usually recommend psychiatrists for counseling (unless they are a psychoanalytic practitioner in which case they may be ideal for exploring the types of issues raised in Chapter 5). In the United States, psychiatrists are medical doctors (MD) or doctors of osteopathy (DO) and most of them prescribe and monitor medications for the treatment of psychiatric illness; therapy isn't usually their specialty. However, psychiatrists are the best professionals to see if you want to use medication for anxiety, depression, or other mental health conditions that make it difficult for you to change your relationship with helping and giving. Sometimes we need to "clear up" enough that we can do emotional and relational work required to make important changes. [90]

Finding the therapist that's the best fit for you may take a few tries, but it's worth the effort since it can save you a lot of time and pain in the long run. Therapists, like all other people, vary quite a bit and who works for you may be different than who works for someone else. Sometimes it even makes sense to work with one therapist for a while, and when that work is no longer productive, to switch to another.

Concluding Words

As we conclude our journey, I want to say one final time that helping and giving are good. Although there's always a risk our helping and giving may go awry, the benefits of being a helpful and giving person make those risks worth taking. Helping one another really does make the world a better place. People sometimes need our help to overcome undeserved hardship or to change their lives. With our support, determined, persistent people achieve their life goals. A circle of giving in a group or community insures the success of individuals and groups. Good organizational citizens promote productivity and contribute to positive workplace environments. Helping and giving can provide life with meaning and purpose and can boost our mood, express our values, and connect us to something greater than ourselves. It's the outpouring of help following tragedy that gives us hope and the courage to carry on. Giving too little is as bad as giving too much.

Mastering the fine art of helping and giving will serve you well. After all, we're all regularly presented with opportunities for helping and giving and we all face occasional helping and giving relationship challenges. So, I think that it's best to help and give regularly and with an open heart, hoping and expecting the best, but prepared to act when the signs of unhealthy helping and giving are revealed.

Endnotes

1. See N. Weinstein and R. M. Ryan's 2010 article, "When helping helps: autonomous motivation for prosocial behavior and its influence on well-being for the helper and recipient. *Journal of Personality and Social Psychology, volume 98*, pages 222-244.

2. See L.A. Penner, J.F. Dovidio, J. A. Piliavin, and D. A. Schroeder's 2006 chapter "Prosocial behavior: Multilevel perspectives" in the *Annual Review of Psychology, volume 56*, pages 365-392.

Chapter 1 – Understanding the Difference Between Healthy and Unhealthy Helping

3. Hazelton Publishing (2013).

4. See G.E. Dear, C. M Roberts, & L. Lange, (2005) "Defining Codependency: A Thematic Analysis of Published Definitions" in *Advances in Psychology*, volume 34, pages 189-205.

5. See James Andrew Hogg and Mary Lou Frank (1992), "Toward an Interpersonal Model of Codependence and Contradependence," in the *Journal of Counseling & Development,* volume 70, pages 371-375.

6. See for example, N.D. Reyome, K.S. Ward, and K. Witkiewitz (2010) "Childhood Emotional Maltreatment and Later Intimate Relationships: Themes From the Empirical Literature" in the *Journal of Aggression, Maltreatment & Trauma*, volume 19, pages 224-242.

Chapter 2 – Unhealthy Helping & Giving Relationships

7. "What We Spend," *AARP: The Magazine* (August/September 2013), p. 54.

8. Many people with serious addictions act like personality-disordered individuals but once sober their "old" personality returns and they

desire independence. Of course, some personality-disordered individuals (especially anti-social and borderline personalities) are prone to drug and alcohol abuse. They will remain difficult takers even when "clean."

9. The DSM is published by the American Psychiatric Association. A sixth edition was published in 2013.

10. When I shared this observation with my husband he suggested that I call them the "enabling chain gang."

11. Of course, takers can have multiple dysfunctional helpers as well.

Chapter 3 – The Negative Consequences of Unhealthy Helping & Giving

12. If you've started thinking that maybe you'd rather be dead, call the toll-free, 24-hour hotline of the National Suicide Prevention Lifeline at 1-800-273-TALK (1-800-273-8255); TTY: 1-800-799-4TTY (4889) to talk to a trained counselor. Or, call your doctor, dial 911, or go to the emergency room. For a detailed booklet on depression and its treatment, go to http://www.nimh.nih.gov/health/publications/depression/complete-index.shtml.

13. C.R. Figley (2002). Compassion fatigue: Psychotherapists' chronic lack of self care. *Journal of Clinical Psychology*, volume *58*, pages1433-1441.

14. Compassion fatigue and secondary trauma are typically discussed within the context of professional helpers, such as psychotherapists, social workers, sexual assault counselors, and rescue workers but I believe they apply to non-professional helpers as well.

15. Albert Bandura (1982). Self-efficacy mechanism in human agency. *American Psychologist*, volume 37, pages 122-147.

16. J.S. Adams (1965). Inequity in social exchange. In *Advances in Experimental Social Psychology*, volume 62, pages 335-343.

17. Edward W. Miles, John D. Hatfield, and Richard C. Huseman (1994). "Equity sensitivity and outcome importance." *Journal of Organizational Behavior,* volume 15, pages 585-596.

18. A. Nadler & J.D. Fisher (1986) in *Advances in Experimental Social Psychology (Vol. 19)*, Editor L. Berkowitiz.

19. Arie Nadler and Samer Halabi (2006) talk about how assumptive help can imply the beneficiary's low status. See "Intergroup Helping As Status Relations: Effects of Status Stability, Identification, and Type of Help on Receptivity to High-status Group's Help." *Journal of Personality and Social Psychology, volume* 91, pages 97-110.

20. This explanation for slacking on group tasks comes from the collective effort model of social loafing created by social psychologists S.J. Karau and J.D. Williams (1993).

21. In the study of group dynamics, the slacking of group members is called "social loafing." The person that gets stuck doing a disproportionate amount of the group's work is called a "sucker," the slacking members are called "free riders," and when the sucker starts withholding effort because they're sick of doing all the work it's called the "sucker effect."

22. See Grant's book *Give and Take: A Revolutionary Approach to Success* published in 2013 by Viking Adult.

Chapter 4 – The Personality Traits of Unhealthy Helpers & Givers

23. C. Peterson & M. Seligman (2004). *Character Strengths and Virtues: A Handbook and Classification.* American Psychological Association and Oxford University Press.

24. L. A. Penner and H. Orom's (2010) "Enduring goodness: A person-by-situation perspective on prosocial behavior" in *Prosocial Motives, Emotions, and Behavior: The Better Angels of Our Nature* edited by M. Mikulincer and P.R. Shaver. Washington, DC, American Psychological Association.

25. Some people with this personality orientation may focus on the welfare and rights of animals. They feel strong concern and empathy for animal suffering, and act to rescue and save them.

26. E. Midlarsky, S. Fagin Jones, & R. P. Corley (2005). Personality correlates of heroic rescue during the Holocaust. *Journal of Personality*, volume 73, pages 907-934.

27. See for example, J.M. Digman (1990). Personality structure: Emergence of the Five Factor Model. *Annual Review of Psychology*, volume 41, pages 417–440.

28. W. Graziano, M.Habashi, B. Sheese, and R. Tobin (2007). "Agreeableness, Empathy, and Helping: A Person × Situation Perspective." *Journal of Personality and Social Psychology*, volume 93, pages 583-600.

29. See for example, research by Jack W. Berry and his colleagues (2001) on dispositional forgiveness in the journal *Personality and Social Psychology Bulletin*, volume 27, pages 1277-1290.

30. Some researchers (like Nancy Eisenberg and her colleagues) use the term "sympathy" instead of empathy.

31. See for example, a 1989 article by Nancy Eisenberg and her colleagues, "The Role of Sympathy and Altruistic Personality Traits in Helping: A Reexamination" in the *Journal of Personality, volume 57*, pages 41-67.

32. See S. Gaertner and J. Dovidio's "The arousal cost-reward model and the process of intervention: A review of the evidence" in the 1991 book *Prosocial Behavior: Review of Personality and Social Psychology, Vol. 12* edited by Margaret Clark (Sage Publications).

33. For a summary of research see C. Daniel Batson and Adam A. Powell's "Altruism and prosocial behavior" in the *Handbook of Psychology* (2003).

34. Even non-human animals are more likely to help relatives and members of their group over nonrelatives and strangers. Some theorists speculate that helping others is an inborn tendency (innate) because it contributes to the survival of tribes and species.

35. Social psychologist Bernard Weiner originated the idea that we make attributions about the worthiness of the victim and that these affect our willingness to help.

36. Don't get me wrong—in a just and humanitarian world, people with disabilities receive needed accommodations so that they may live their lives to the fullest extent possible. I'm just saying people with disabilities are in some danger of having loved ones and caregivers underestimate their abilities and foster dependency with their help, rather than independence and autonomy.

37. Widiger and Presnall's chapter on this topic can be found in the 2011 book *Pathological Altruism* edited by Barbara Oakley, Ariel Knafo, Guruprasad Madhavan, and David Sloan Wilson (Oxford University Press).

38. See for example, Paul Costa and Thomas A.Widiger's (2012) book, *Personality Disorders and the Five-factor Model of Personality* published by the American Psychiatric Association.

39. B. M. Le, E. A. Impett, A. Kogan, G. D. Webster, and C. Cheng, (2013), "The personal and interpersonal rewards of communal orientation." In the *Journal of Social and Personal Relationships, volume 30*, pages 694-710.

40. G. V. Caprara and P. Steca (2005). "Self–efficacy beliefs as determinants of prosocial behavior conducive to life satisfaction across ages." *Journal of Social and Clinical Psychology, volume 24*, pages 191-217.

41. Festinger first published this theory in the journal *Human Relations* in a 1954 article called "A Theory of Social Comparison Processes" (*volume 7*, pages 117-140).

42. We used a statistical procedure called regression analysis to determine this. At the time of this writing, the study was recently completed and had not been submitted it for publication consideration.

43. See the 1991 article "Evidence of codependency in women with an alcoholic parent: Helping out Mr. Wrong," by D. Lyon and J. Greenberg, in the *Journal of Personality and Social Psychology*, (volume 61, pages 435-439).

44. J. Crocker and L. E. Park, (2004). "The costly pursuit of self-esteem." *Psychological Bulletin, volume 130*, pages 392-414.

45. An excellent self-help workbook that may help with low self-esteem is *Ten Days to Self-Esteem* by psychiatrist David D. Burns.

Chapter 5 _ Unconscious and Emotional Influences on Unhealthy Helping & Giving

46. See Jay R. Goldberg and Stephen A. Mitchell's 1983 book *Object Relations in Psychoanalytic Theory* published by Harvard University Press.

47. Funny story: I worked on this book for over a year before realizing I had a serious problem with dysfunctional helping and giving. It is now

obvious that I was drawn to this project partly for my own unconscious reasons.

48. Sigmund Freud, "The economic problem of masochism," in *The Standard Edition of the Complete Psychological Works of Sigmund Freud, Volume XIX (1923-1925): The Ego and the Id and Other Works* (pp. 155-170). Published by Hogarth in 1961.

49. Anna Freud, "The Ego *and* the Mechanisms of Defense: The Writings of Anna Freud." Published by International Universities Press in 1979.

50. I *would* look at the id, ego, and superego metaphorically, not literally.

51. The *PDM* was authored by the PDM Task Force (2006) and published by the Alliance of Psychoanalytic Organizations, Silver Springs, Maryland. Earlier in the book we talked about personality disorders described in the *DSM* (the Diagnostic and *Statistical* Manual of Mental Disorders published by the American Psychiatric Association). Unlike the PDM, which is based in psychoanalytic theory, the DSM does not speculate about the causes of the disorders it describes; its goal is simply the classification of various mental disorders and their diagnostic criteria. It is more widely used by physicians and mental health professionals, especially since insurance companies typically require DSM codes to pay for treatment.

52. See Karen Horney's *Our Inner Conflicts: A Constructive Theory Of Neurosis* published in 1945 by W.W. Norton and reissued in 1992 in a paperback version.

53. Pointing out the silliness of this kind of thinking and putting it to the test, as I suggest here, are more consistent with the cognitive behavioral approach discussed in Chapter 10 than the psychoanalytic/psychodynamic approach. However, I didn't want to make you wait for some common sense that might help.

Chapter 6 _ Family Influences: Learning Codependence and Bad Helping Habits

54. Bandura, A. (1977). *Social Learning Theory*. Englewood Cliffs, NJ: Prentice Hall.

55. See for example, Philippe J. Rushton's (1982) *Social Learning Theory and the Development of Prosocial Behavior* (Academic Press).

56. See Albert Bandura (2001) "Social Cognitive Theory: An Agentic Perspective" in the *Annual Review of Psychology, Volume 52,* pages 1-26.

57. Kahneman's book "Thinking Fast and Thinking Slow" (2011 Macmillan Books), describes these two cognitive (thinking) systems, one automatic and one conscious, and their implications for everyday life and decision-making.

58. See John Bowlby's 1973 book, *Attachment and Loss: Separation: Anxiety and Anger (volume 2)*. Basic Books.

59. For more detail, see Shelley A. Riggs (2010), "Childhood Emotional Abuse and the Attachment System Across the Life Cycle: What Theory and Research Tell Us." *Journal of Aggression, Maltreatment & Trauma*, volume 19, pages 5-51.

60. For a history and summary of this work see Hector Mikulincer and Phillip R. Shaver's 2010 book, *Attachment in Adulthood: Structure, Dynamics, and Change*. Guilford Press.

61. See B.F. Skinner's 1976 book *About Behaviorism* (published by Vintage) for an understandable presentation of his main ideas.

62. Robert Cialdini, B. Robert, Stephanie L. Brown, Brian P. Lewis, Carol Luce, and Steven L. Neuberg (1997). "Reinterpreting the empathy–altruism relationship: When one into one equals oneness." *Journal of Personality and Social Psychology, volume 73*, pages 481-494.

63. It should be noted that Cialdini didn't present his theory as a behavioral theory but it makes sense that helper's high could positively reinforce dysfunctional helping.

64. See the book *Pathological Altruism* (2011; Oxford University Press), edited by Barbara Oakley.

Chapter 7 – The Cognitive Roots of Unhealthy Helping & Giving

65. See Ellis's classic books *The New Guide to Rational Living* (Wilshire Book Co; 3rd edition 1975), and *Reason and Emotion in Psychotherapy* (Citadel, 1974).

66. I often recommend that people chant Reinhold Niebuhr's Serenity Prayer like it's a meditative mantra: "God, grant me the serenity to accept the things I cannot change, courage to change the things I can, and the wisdom to know the difference." Some of you might recognize this from 12-step programs.

67. These are most often described in the context of mood disorders such as depression. For example, see David Burns' 1999 book *Feeling Good: The New Mood Therapy* (Harper Collins Publishers). However, I believe they're applicable here.

Chapter 8 – How Culture & Gender Influence Unhealthy Helping and Giving

68. See for example, the 2013 research article "Friends in high places: The influence of authoritarian and benevolent god-concepts on social attitudes and behaviors" by Kathryn Johnson and her colleagues Jessica Li, Adam Cohen, and Morris Okun in the journal *Psychology Of Religion And Spirituality, volume 5*, pages 15-22.

69. Hazel Markus and Shinobu Kitayama (1991) "Culture and the self: Implications for cognition, emotion, and motivation." In the research journal *Psychological Review,* volume 98, pp. 224-253.

70. The dominant Euro American culture of the United States is largely individualistic but the United States is a multicultural society and some American groups are more collectivistic such as Asian American and Mexican American cultures.

71. S-H Chang (2012), "A Cultural Perspective on Codependency and Its Treatment." In the *Asia Pacific Journal of Counseling and Psychotherapy,* volume 3, pages 50-60.

72. J. Inclan and M. Hernandez (1992). Cross-cultural perspectives and codependence: The case of poor Hispanics. *American Journal of Orthopsychiatry,* volume 62, pages 245-255.

73. According to the US Census (2010), 10 percent of married heterosexual couples, 18 percent of unmarried heterosexual couples, and 21 percent of non-heterosexual couples are interracial couples.

74. See for example W. Graziano, M.Habashi, B. Sheese, and R. Tobin (2007). "Agreeableness, Empathy, and Helping: A Person × Situation Perspective." *Journal of Personality and Social Psychology,* volume 93, pages 583-600.

75. Religious fundamentalisms are committed to the authority of ancient scriptures and believe them to be infallible; they tend to idealize a past where gender spheres were separate and men and women's roles were distinct. They tend to promote the idea that women's primary role should be one of service as traditional wife and mother.

76. G. Cowan and L.W. Warren (1994), "Codependency and gender-stereotyped traits." *Sex Roles,* volume 30, pages 631-645.

77. G. Noriega, L. Ramos, M.E. Medina-Mora, and A.R. & Villa, A. R. (2008). "Prevalence of codependence in young women seeking primary health care and associated risk factors." *American Journal of Orthopsychiatry*, volume 78, pages 199-209.

78. See G.E. Dear and C.M. Roberts (2002). "The relationships between codependency and femininity and masculinity." In *Sex Roles: A Journal of Research*, volume 46, pages 159-165.

79. See S-H Chang (2012), "A Cultural Perspective on Codependency and Its Treatment." *Asia Pacific Journal of Counseling and Psychotherapy,* volume 3, pages 50-60.

80. S-H Chang (2012), "A Cultural Perspective on Codependency and Its Treatment." *Asia Pacific Journal of Counseling and Psychotherapy,* volume 3, pages 50-60.

81. This means that the previous paragraphs about culture and dysfunctional helping are vast over-simplifications.

Chapter 9 – Healthy Helping & Giving Boundary Setting

82. Called *Your Perfect Right: Assertiveness and Equality in Your Life and Relationships,* a ninth edition was published in 2008 by Impact Publishing in Atascadero, California.

83. Published by William Morrow Paperbacks.

84. These are based on the constructive confrontation guidelines described by Robert Kolt and William Donohue in their 1992 book, *Managing Interpersonal Conflict* published by Sage.

85. In the *Dance of Intimacy.*

Chapter 10 – Conclusion

86. Developed by James Prochaska and Wayne Velicer (1997). See "The transtheoretical model of health behavior change" in the *American Journal of Health Promotion,* volume 12, pages 38-48.

87. In the United States, you can call the National Domestic Violence Hotline for assistance: 1-800-799-7233 or TTY 1-800-787-3224. http://www.thehotline.org

88. MI is a bona fide, psychologist-approved acronym that has appeared on many PowerPoint slides. It is frequently bandied about by small packs of helping professionals drinking at the coffee hole. For more information about MI, see W.R. Miller and S. Rollick's *Motivational Interviewing: Preparing People for Change* (Guilford Press, 2002).

89. How many psychologists does it take to change a light bulb? One. But the light bulb has to want to change.

90. Medication affects each person differently and a good psychiatrist will work with you to find the medication and dosage that makes you feel better with the fewest side effects. In comparison to other medical doctors, they're experts about the medications used to treat these types of conditions. If possible, see a psychiatrist rather than another type of medical doctor for medications for the treatment of mental health conditions.